The Best Plays From
The Strawberry One-Act Festival
Volume Eight

The Best Plays From
The Strawberry One-Act Festival
Volume Eight

Compiled by Van Dirk Fisher

The Best Plays From The Strawberry One-Act Festival Volume Eight
Compiled by Van Dirk Fisher

iUniverse books may be ordered through booksellers or by contacting:

iUniverse
1663 Liberty Drive
Bloomington, IN 47403
www.iuniverse.com
1-800-Authors (1-800-288-4677)

ISBN: 978-1-4917-8452-5 (sc)
ISBN: 978-1-4917-8454-9 (e)

Library of Congress Control Number: 2015920228

Print information available on the last page.

iUniverse rev. date: 12/17/2015

The Best Plays From The Strawberry One-Act Festival
Volume Eight
Compiled by Van Dirk Fisher

**THE
STRAWBERRY
ONE-ACT
FESTIVAL**

www.TheRiantTheatre.com

Welcome to the 8th Volume of the Best Plays From The Strawberry One-Act Festival. **The Strawberry One-Act Festival**, which began in 1995 in New York City, is the brainchild of The Riant Theatre's Artistic Director, Van Dirk Fisher. The festival is a play competition in which the audience and the theatre's judges cast their votes to select the best play of the season.

Twice a year, hundreds of plays from across the country are submitted for the competition, of which 40 are chosen to compete. Plays move from the 1st round to the semi-finals and then the finals. The playwright of the winning play receives a grant and the opportunity to have a full-length play developed by the Riant. In addition, awards are given out for Best Director, Best Actor and Best Actress.

During the year 2015 the Winter and Summer Strawberry One-Act Festival streamed online and were made available for viewing worldwide on Video On Demand. You can visit our website to view the plays On Demand on Vimeo as well as subscribe to see several plays from the Strawberry One-Act Festival VOD HD for a nominal monthly subscription fee. Visit www.therianttheatre.com for more details.

This anthology includes plays from the Summer of 2012 through the Winter of 2015. The Strawberry One-Act Festival is a wonderful opportunity for the audience and the industry alike to see some of the best talent in the nation. Every performance features three to four dynamic one-act plays. There's always a lot of buzz surrounding each performance as artists converge and network on future projects. Several of the playwrights whose plays are featured in the festival have written for the literary world, as well as for television and film. "We are very fortunate to be able to fulfill our mission, which is to discover and develop talent and playwrights for the stage," says Mr. Fisher. "We are very proud of this accomplishment, but the work doesn't stop there. Competition aside, everyone's a winner in the festival, because several actors, directors and playwrights are chosen to work on future projects at the Riant."

During the Winter 2012 Festival, the audience's votes – as well as those of the playwrights in attendance -- selected *THE EXIT INTERVIEW* by Betsy Kagen and MK Walsh as the Best Play of the Season. The winner of the Summer 2012 Festival was *FOOTHOLD* by Patrick J. Lennon.

The first play in this anthology is *FOOTHOLD* by Patrick J. Lennon, in which a goofy Mary Poppins-ish nurse treats a shy man with an ingrown toenail and a broken heart. I love this charming play. It was definitely a crowd pleaser.

Things get messy when you're the subject of your own story. In *WRITERS RETREAT* by Samantha Ciavarella, two friends/lovers/writers discover that they cannot have their cake and eat it too as they spend a weekend in a cabin working. This play will take you on a rollercoaster of emotions as these two people learn the true value of their relationship. This Best Play nominee garnered the Best Actor Award for Andrew Schoomaker.

A SONG A DAY KEEPS THE DOCTOR AWAY by Freddy Valle, was a finalist in the Winter 2015 festival. The play is a hilarious situation comedy that had the audiences falling out of their seats with laughter. A woman takes her boyfriend to see his doctor to help him with a very embarrassing predicament that happens every time he opens his mouth to speak. The fun part is trying to cure him of his ailment. Hold on tight. It's going to be a bumpy ride.

Often playwrights are inspired by real life experiences to write their plays. Hollywood screenwriter and first time playwright David E. Tolchinsky found much success with his play *WHERE'S THE REST OF ME?*, in which a screenwriter wrestles with his relationship to Spalding Gray, his psychiatrist father and the classic movie *King's Row*. The play is a dark and funny journey through movies, monologues and mental illness. Mr. Tolchinsky won the Best Director Award with this play.

Too often in life teenagers who have serious problems are easily dismissed as "teen angst." In Rachel Robyn Wagner's play *KIDS THESE DAYS,* five Boston High School students open up to each other and reveal their darkest secrets after they stumble upon a diary accidently left behind by a fellow classmate. This powerful play is a wakeup call to all of us that it's important for us to pay attention to each other and to show some compassion. Everybody has a story. You never know what a person is going through if you don't take the time to ask.

Keaton Weiss' play HOPELESS, IRRESISTIBLE deals with people in their afterlife. Two strangers meet at a mysterious train station in an ambiguous afterlife, and force each other to confront their tragic pasts and shape their uncertain futures. This dark drama unfolds with intrigue that is spellbinding.

Working in the healthcare profession can be very taxing and stressful. In Phoebe Farber's play HOME CARE, a nurse is suspended for attacking a colleague and is forced to attend therapy to deal with her anger. This play was a finalist in the festival.

THE EXIT INTERVIEW by Betsy Kagen and MK Walsh is a comedy that won the Best Play Award in the Winter Festival of 2012. Before moving onto the afterlife, a young woman must participate in an exit interview with an obnoxious celestial being.

PAULA'S VISITOR by Keith Miles Filangieri, centers on the dynamics of two couples on a tour of the South African jungle. Newlyweds Lana and Freddy seem to be enchanted with the exoticism of their honeymoon spot, as well as with each other, while Paula and Jim have four years of marriage (and more than the beginnings of disillusionment) under their belts. Neither couple will escape unchanged after this excursion.

The last play in this anthology is the comedy ABRAMOVIĆ by Kory French. As middle America continues with its economic struggles, a MOMA – visiting Midwestern twenty-something tries to understand the monetary value of high-art, grounding his friend in the process.

I hope that you enjoy these plays as much as I have with the hundreds of people who have seen them in the Strawberry One-Act Festival. Share them with your friends and family. If they make you laugh or cry, entertain you or even enlighten you in any way, then I guess they have served their purpose: to touch people's souls.

Enjoy them and if you're ever in New York City be sure to check out the Strawberry One-Act Festival. But if you can't make it to NYC, please check out several of the plays On Demand. Visit www.therianttheatre. com for further details. In addition, you can check out The Video Diaries Project: A Series of Short Films about the Artists in the Strawberry One-Act Festival. You can view the short films for free on our website www.

therianttheatre.com and get information on other plays and workshops we produce. Please follow us on Twitter at www.twitter.com/RiantTheatre and on Facebook at www.facebook.com/RiantTheatre and www.facebook.com/StrawberryOneActFestival. And know that at the Riant Theatre you are always welcome, welcome, WELCOME!

Van Dirk Fisher
Founder & Artistic Director
The Riant Theatre
P.O. Box 1902
New York, NY 10013
RiantTheatre@gmail.com

To hear some great music go to www.cdbaby.com/cd/toejambeats or www.myspace.com/toejambeats419 or www.myspace.com/lovingyouthemusical

Table of Contents

FOOTHOLD

written by Patrick J. Lennon
directed by Richard E. Knipe, Jr.
with
Alison Bernhardt & George Raboni

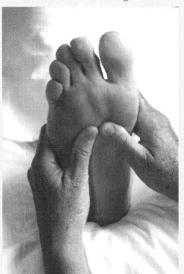

STRAWBERRY ONE-ACT FESTIVAL 2012
The Theater at St. Clements
423 West 46th Street, NYC

FOOTHOLD by Patrick J. Lennon

FOOTHOLD

By Patrick J. Lennon

Patrick J. Lennon is a Masters in Creative Writing Graduate from the City University of New York – Queens College. A former English teacher at Roosevelt Jr.-Sr. High School in Roosevelt, NY, he is Co-Founder of Tiger's Heart Players in Croton-on-Hudson, NY and the Founder/President of the Aery Theatre Company in Garrison, NY. His plays have been produced Off-Off-Broadway and Off-Broadway.

Foothold made its New York City debut in August 2012 at the Riant Theatre in the Strawberry One-Act Festival, where it won the Best Play Award, with the following cast, in order of appearance:

MARY   Alison Bernhardt (nominee – Best Actress)
THOMAS WELLS   George Raboni (nominee – Best Actor)

The play was directed by Richard Edwin Knipe, Jr.

CAST OF CHARACTERS

Mary, 30-ish, female podiatrist's assistant. Goofy, Mary Poppins-like. Thomas Wells, 60-ish, in-grown toenail patient. A sad sack, nervous-type.

(Time is the present, between Christmas and New Year's. The place is a podiatrist's office in Rockland County, NY. At rise, Thomas enters a dimly lit waiting room, walking gingerly, with the aid of a cane. He looks around, then sits. Mary enters in scrubs, the blouse with a bold Tweety Bird design.)

MARY: Greetings.
THOMAS: I'm here to see Dr. Buzzollo.
MARY: You have an appointment – Mr...?
THOMAS: Wells.

MARY: Well then welcome, Mr. Wells. *(Laughs.)* Oh, that kinda rhymes, doesn't it? No it doesn't. Come in, please.
(Mary retreats behind a counter/desk. Slips on a pair of large-framed glasses without lenses and begins fiddling through an appointment book.)
MARY: *(cont'd)* Let's have a looksee.
THOMAS: A looksee? *(Noticing her glasses.)* Do those have lenses?
MARY: No, no – I just always liked the way I looked in glasses – though they don't help me see. What do you think?
(She looks back to the appointment book.)
MARY: *(cont'd)* I don't find you…
THOMAS: 2:15.
MARY: Who did you speak with?
THOMAS: I don't remember.
MARY: Mary?
THOMAS: I might have spoken with a Mary.
MARY: That's me! I'm the only Mary! But still, I don't see…
THOMAS: I'm sure it was today… *(Looking over her shoulder.)* Your computer's not on.
MARY: Oops! Wait. No – here it is. Wells… is it Thomas? *(Thomas nods.)* Can't understand this scribble. It's like a doctor's subscription.
THOMAS: Thank God. The thought of actually coming here and… *(Beat.)* Wait, did you say "subscription"?
MARY: Yes.
THOMAS: But it's…
MARY: I know. *(Beat.)* So you're his 2:15. Wait, I have to do this.
(Mary taps on her stapler, as if it's an intercom button.)
MARY: *(cont'd)* Dr. B – your 2:15 is here.
(Thomas looks at her quizzically.)
MARY: *(cont'd)* I know – there's no intercom. I just like doing that. *(Pressing the imaginary button again, in a deep voice.)* "Uh, Mary – would you hold all my calls, please?" I love those scenes in the old movies – don't you? *(Beat.)* Anyway, Dr. B stepped out for lunch. He'll be back shortly.
THOMAS: I am a little early.
MARY: You're too young to be that old.
THOMAS: What?
MARY: You know how old people come to doctor's appointments an hour and a half early? Just to make sure, y'know? You're too young to buy into that.

THOMAS: I turned 60 in October.

MARY: Really? You don't look it. I would have said late teens.

THOMAS: You wouldn't say that if you saw my joints.

MARY: *(Feigning offense.)* Excuse me?

THOMAS: *(Flustered, frantically pointing to his knees and hips.)* I – I'm sorry. I was referring to…

MARY: *(Laughing.)* I was just playing with you. *(Noticing Thomas' gloves.)* Did you ride here?

THOMAS: Ride?

MARY: Motorcycle.

THOMAS: Me? No. Why do you ask?

MARY: The gloves. The black gear. I imagine you pulling in on a softail – or maybe a fatboy. Yeah, fatboy – that's it.

THOMAS: I don't even know what those are.

MARY: Oh, man – I love bikes. *(Beat.)* Hey – so does Lauren Hutton – y'know, the movie star? Nearly died in a bike accident a few years ago. Do you know that if Lauren Hutton married Kevin Hutton, the motorcycle racer, she'd become Mrs. Lauren Hutton Hutton… hutton, vroom, hutton vroom, hutton vroom vroom *(holding onto imaginary handlebars and making motorcycle sounds. Mary laughs at her own joke. Thomas stares, unbelieving, then breaks into a smile.)*

MARY: I know, I'm a piece of work – that's what everyone says – though I prefer to think of myself as a piece of work in progress. I like that better, Thomas.

MARY: *(cont'd, almost in a secret whisper)* And I like Thomas better than Mr. Wells – don't you? Still, I don't understand you being dressed in all black, if you're not a biker. Unless… *(Beat.)* Oh – oh, I apologize. I'm sorry for your loss.

THOMAS: My loss?

MARY: Well, have you lost someone recently?

THOMAS: NO!

MARY: Then I'm not sorry for your loss! Anyway, as I said, Dr. B stepped out for lunch, so let's get you prepped. I love that word – "prepped." It sounds so medically "with it." Now, I'll just grab your file. Follow me. *(Beat.)* I notice your cane. Does that have anything to do with why you're here?

THOMAS: No – that's something different. I had both hips replaced last year. There were complications. They're taking longer than I thought to heal.

MARY: I'm sorry. There I go – sorry again. But I am sorry you're hurting. It pains me to see you walk. *(Beat.)* So, Thomas – see, I'm getting used to it already – what brings you here – a follow up? A new issue?

THOMAS: Uh – new issue… I guess.

MARY: And that is?

THOMAS: *(Uncomfortably.)* Ingrown toenail.

MARY: Oooh, we get a lot of those. Which one?

THOMAS: The… the big one.

MARY: The one who went to the market?

THOMAS: 'Scuse me?

MARY: It was the piggy who went to the market.

THOMAS: *(Glancing around.)* Do you actually work here?

MARY: Tsk – of course I work here. *(Gesturing to her Tweety Bird scrub blouse. Sing-songy.)* Hello! Now which one?

THOMAS: *(Reluctantly.)* The one… who went to the market.

MARY: And the other piggies – they're fine?

THOMAS: *(With a touch of annoyance.)* Yes – all the other piggies are fine. I can't believe we're having this conversation.

MARY: Why?

THOMAS: For one, being in a podiatrist's examination room and talking about which little piggy hurts.

MARY: Should I have asked you which piggy hurts out in the office – where everyone could hear?

THOMAS: But there was no one else out there.

MARY: There was you and me, Thomas – we'd have heard.

THOMAS: But that's not even the point.

MARY: What is the point?

THOMAS: I don't understand why you'd call them Piggies. This is a podiatrist's office – not a pediatrician's office. Aren't you supposed to call them something like…

MARY: … more grown up?

THOMAS: Exactly.

MARY: Why?

THOMAS: I don't know – it'd make me feel more comfortable, for one.

MARY: Well, then would hallux work better for you?

THOMAS: Hallux?

MARY: It's the medical term for the big toe.

THOMAS: I know. I…

MARY: Thomas, let's say you have hallux rigidis – your big toe is stiff. Believe me, a lotta people come in with that, too. It's bad enough you have pain – and have to go to a doctor. Why do they need to use scary words? Don'tcha think a patient would feel better if he was told he had a stiff piggy? Much less threatening, I'd say. *(Beat.)* Hallux Rigidus – always made me think of a strict Catholic school. "Where did you go to high school?" "Me? Albertus Magnus. What about you?" "Oh, I went to… Hallux Rigidis." "Whoa, nuns there were tough, weren't they?" "The worst."

(Brief silence.)

MARY: I went to North Rockland.

THOMAS: Not Albertus Magnus?

MARY: Me? Tsk – I don't think so.

THOMAS: Why?

MARY: I wasn't in that league.

THOMAS: My parents sent me away to a military prep school outside Philadelphia.

MARY: Aha! A discipline problem!

THOMAS: Hardly. My father went to military prep school – so I was sent to military prep school. "It makes a man out of you."

MARY: Your words – or his?

THOMAS: *(Sarcastically.)* Ha!

MARY: What was it called?

THOMAS: What?

MARY: The military prep school that made a man out of you. What was it called?

THOMAS: It was called… Flexus Biceptus.

MARY: *(Laughing.)* You're funny, Thomas. But I'd say you need to laugh more.

THOMAS: What is there to laugh about?

MARY: You need to look harder.

THOMAS: I really doubt that would matter.

MARY: So I guess you're a doubting Thomas then.

THOMAS: I doubt that.

MARY: *(Laughing.)* You doubt you're a doubting Thomas? Whew! Then a little more faith would help as well. *(Looking at her bare wrist.)*

Okay, the doctor will be here in about 20 minutes, so let's get you prepar… prepped. Take off your shoes and socks, and sit here in this chair. I'll go get your footbath ready.

(Mary leaves. Backstage she's heard singing "Splish, splash, I was takin' a bath…". Thomas bends, trying desperately to reach the laces on his shoes. He tries again with his cane, but to no avail. Mary returns shortly with a foot bowl.)

MARY *(cont'd)* Let's get those shoes and…

THOMAS: That's, uh, a little bit of a problem. I have some trouble getting them off. I can't bend my hip – you know, to reach down there.

MARY: Your shoes and socks?

THOMAS: Yes – basically.

MARY: OK – no problemo.

(Mary crouches down.)

THOMAS: Just… be gentle. Sometimes a quick movement will make me jerk…

MARY: Don't worry. That's what Mary is best at – gentle.

(She unties both shoes and gently slips them off. She removes his socks.)

MARY *(cont'd. She drops the socks in the foot bowl.)* How do you get them on?

THOMAS: Ah – this gadget they gave me when I was discharged. It's a reacher/grasper thing. So aggravating – like trying to pick something up when your hand's asleep. You know those things in the arcade that have the mechanical claw to pick up the prize…

MARY: The prize that costs less than what you pay to play the game…

THOMAS: Exactly. Just when you think you have it, it drops out of the claw…

(Mary takes hold of his one foot and, with one finger, traces a heart just below his ankle.)

THOMAS: Why did you do that?

MARY: What?

THOMAS: You traced something on my foot.

MARY: It's my signature.

THOMAS: No, it wasn't a signature. It was a heart, wasn't it?

MARY: Yes.

THOMAS: Why?

MARY: To help the healing.

THOMAS: But that's not where it hurts.

MARY: Oh… It spreads.

THOMAS: It does.

MARY: Love heals.

THOMAS: Love heals?

MARY: Precisely.

THOMAS: You believe that?

MARY: I wouldn't be here if I didn't.

THOMAS: I don't think my wife believes that.

MARY: Your wife? Oh, your wife!

THOMAS: Oh, Jeez – here we go. *(Beat.)* She lost her father a few years ago. Fed him, dressed him, washed him – the whole deal. Then, after my operations – I mean, I'm not getting any better, Mary – I'm getting worse. Christ, I'm only 60. I don't think she can handle that again.

MARY: "In sickness and in health," Thomas.

THOMAS: Look at me… willya look at me? I used to run. I used to play tennis, Goddammit! We were supposed to go to Tuscany, you know!? Walk the hillside! *(Laughs.)* Hillside – my ass! I can't walk a block without pain. *(Beat.)* I told her to go by herself.

MARY: And she took you up on it.

THOMAS: Yeah, she took me up on it!

MARY: Did you say it nice?

THOMAS: Nice?

MARY: Yeah – nice. Did you tell her she should walk the hillside of Tuscany by herself nice?

THOMAS: I don't even know what that means! I just told her she should go by herself.

MARY: Didya meant it?

THOMAS: I said it, didn't I? For Chrissakes, what d'ya want from me?

MARY: So you were okay with her going – by herself?

THOMAS: Jesus – she needed it. I know she did. But the timing – y'know… I wanted her to go… no, I wanted her to know that she could go – that I was fine with it – even happy for her.

MARY: To walk the hillsides of Tuscany without you.

THOMAS: Yes… no… I DON'T KNOW!!! Maybe I was hoping she'd say she'd rather wait for me.

MARY: *(After a bit.)* But she didn't.

THOMAS: No.

(Mary moves pensively.)

MARY: So… you had control of the prize. It didn't "drop out of the claw". You could have pulled it in, but instead… you let it go. *(Pause.)* You didn't lose it, Thomas - you just did the loving, caring thing – to let the one you love the most be free. A wise choice, I'd say. A very wise choice.

(Mary lifts Thomas' feet and gently places them in the foot bowl, squeezing a water-soaked sponge over them. There is momentary silence, save for the trickling of water. Shortly, she picks up a towel from her lap and begins to dry his feet. Then, placing one in her lap, she again traces a heart.)

THOMAS: You really think so.

MARY: Oh, most indubitably. Hopefully, she gets a grip. Get it – grip? *(Beat.)* Now – you sit down and make yourself comfy till the doctor comes. And don't let him use any of those scary words on you.

(Mary rises, dries her hands and sets the towels on the counter. She reaches in her pocket and withdraws an oversized rainbow lollipop, handing it to him. She then turns and begins to move toward the doorway. Thomas looks up.)

THOMAS: Mary?

MARY: Yes?

THOMAS: Thanks.

MARY: You're welcome.

THOMAS: No, I mean… *(He makes a heart sign with two fingers.)* …thanks.

(Mary smiles. She moves into the reception office area as the lights dim on Thomas to darkness and come up full on Mary. The phone rings.)

MARY: *(Picking up the phone.)* Rockland Foot Fairies… just kidding… Dr. Buzzolo's office. *(Laughing, then listening.)* Oh, we get a lot of those. *(Pause.)* Just so I can note your file… is it the one that got roast beef, or the one that got none?

(She laughs as the lights fade.)

THE END

Samantha Ciavarella *as JO* and Andrew Schoomaker *as BEN*
in WRITERS RETREAT by Samantha Ciavarella.

Writers Retreat

By Sam Ciavarella

Sam Ciavarella is a playwright and comedian originally from New Jersey. She attended the American Musical and Dramatic Academy in NYC and studied improv comedy at the PIT and Upright Citizens Brigade Theater. She is a member of the Dramatist Guild of America, Inc. Her plays, Writers Retreat and Break Room have been featured at The Riant Theatre's Strawberry One-Act Festival and both garnered 'Best Play' nominations.

Writers Retreat began as a way to get back at a boy who broke Sam's heart. Like Taylor Swift, and many other great writers of the day, Sam took her words and used them as weapons developing a story to pull at audiences heartstrings. The outcome was so much more than retaliation when *Writers Retreat* was accepted into the Strawberry One Act Festival during the summer of 2012. During that summer, *Writers Retreat* was performed with the following cast, in order of appearance:

JO: Sam Ciavarella
BEN: Andrew Schoomaker

The play was directed by Kevin Lind.

CAST OF CHARACTERS

JO: early 20's. A New Jersey native and tough as stone. She doesn't have a filter and has a no-bullshit type personality. Among all that strength however, is a sensitive girl just wishing she had the strength to show her more vulnerable side.

BEN: mid 20's. Very good-looking with skin 'the color of wheat' and an all American boy attitude. Ben is from Kansas and is very grass roots in sensibility. Ben has a problem understanding right from wrong and his emotions get in the way of him making sound decisions.

ACT 1
SCENE 1

(Lights up on a motel room. It is tacky and nothing more than two stars in quality. There is a painting of a farm hanging above the queen size bed. There is a desk stage right and a small table stage left. The room almost has a feel of the Bates Motel. The bathroom door, located upstage right, is ajar and we see the light on and hear water running. There is an open laptop on the desk next to the bed. There is also a notebook and a pen next to the laptop. There is a knock on the door. JO, wearing a t-shirt and shorts, comes flying out of the bathroom. She seems anxious. She takes a moment before answering the door to collect herself. She digs through her purse to pull out perfume and sprays some on her.)

    JO: COMING !!!!

(She walks over to the door, calm cool and collected, and opens it. We see BEN standing in the doorway wearing jeans and a Kansas State t-shirt. Without even saying hello he pushes JO into the room and immediately starts to make out with her. These two are animalistic. They are kissing intensely and work their way over to the bed. JO spins BEN around and throws him on the bed. She rips off her shirt and jumps on BEN, straddling him. BEN stares up at JO and the two take a quick moment to breathe. They start kissing again, this time less intense. BEN'S phone rings. He jumps out from underneath JO practically knocking her off the bed. JO lies there impatiently while BEN searches for his phone and answers.)

    BEN: *(on the phone)* Hey baby… yeah I just got here. Jo was here before me so she already started writing. Yeah… Yeah… oh definitely… we're going to get a lot done. Of course babe, I will. But wait babe listen --- I'm gonna turn my phone off okay? We both are. We can't have any outside world distractions while we write. I knew you'd understand. I'll tell Jo you said hi. I'll call you in three days sweetie. I love you too. Bye.

    JO: LOVEEEE when she calls. *(JO gets out of bed and puts her shirt back on. She moves over to the desk and sits at her laptop.)*

    BEN: Don't start Jo.

    JO: Don't start what? Talking about your girlfriend? Or discussing the fact that you tell her you love her while I'm laying here in my bra on the bed?

    BEN: The whole conversation… I don't want to start it again.

    JO: You never do. *(PAUSE)* Who are we writing this screenplay for again?

BEN: It's not a particularly fun topic.

JO: It just makes me feel like shit… that's all I'm trying to say. Do we need to write a comedy or a drama?

BEN: I don't want you to feel like shit.

JO: Then maybe, when she calls, if I'm with you … you could like … go in the bathroom or something… I don't know… whatever …you're right… let's drop it. Can we please focus on writing?

BEN: I didn't think it bothered you.

JO: Honestly, it should bother you. But regardless… I mean …. Doesn't it bother you? To talk to her on the phone right in front of me? Telling her you LOVE her… while you're ten seconds away from ripping the rest of my clothes off? Kind of fucked up… but whatever, that's us I guess…

BEN: Jo, you better stop it.

JO: Writing? Isn't that why we're here?

(BEN gets up and stands behind JO. She is pretending to ignore him. He hovers behind her for a moment and then starts to kiss her neck.)

JO: You are being very unproductive.

BEN: Jo, stop it.

JO: Or what?

BEN: Or I am going to make you stop.

(JO whips her head around and is met by BENS kiss. He pulls her off the chair and tosses her on to the bed. Before she has a moment to collect her thoughts, BEN is on top of her.)

JO: You don't scare me Ben.

BEN: Oh I don't? *(BEN kisses JO hard on the mouth. Without letting go of her arms he starts to kiss her neck… then her clavicle and starts to make his way down to her stomach. She has put her shirt back on at this point so he uses his teeth to pull her shirt up to her tits. He starts kissing her stomach and JO is starting to really get into it. Just as BEN goes to take her pants off, with his mouth, JO resists.)*

JO: OH NO YOU DON'T! I'm still mad at you!

BEN: So punish me.

JO: No, this isn't <u>Fifty Shades of Grey</u>.

BEN: Jo you are fucking killing me.

JO: I'm going to take a shower.

BEN: I'll join you.

JO: Nope… No fun for you.

BEN: What am I supposed to do while you're in the shower?

JO: I mean… you'll have a whole fifteen minutes… so you could just *(indicating masturbation)* …. on your own… I won't even wash my hair so that way you won't have to wait long for me after you finish. *(PAUSE)* Get started on the project we're supposed to write. We are here for a reason other than to fuck each other. It's not like we don't do enough of that in your apartment.

BEN: Very nice. Hurry up.

JO: Yes master.

(Jo strips down to her bra and panties and struts into the bathroom, teasing BEN with every step. BEN sits down at his laptop and starts to write. He sits there quietly writing for a few minutes. Just as we see him start to get in a groove JO emerges from the bathroom in just a towel. She is naked. BEN doesn't even look at her because he is so focused on what he's writing. JO starts digging through her bag to find her pajamas. They remain quiet for a few more minutes. JO goes back into the bathroom and changes. She comes back out of the bathroom in a tight tank top and boy shorts. She doesn't leave much to the imagination.)

JO: How's it going?

BEN: Good.

JO: What are you writing about?

BEN: Two people.

JO: Want to smoke? *(She pulls out weed and a pipe.)*

BEN: Nah… I'm kind of in the zone.

JO: Come on… two minutes... Think about how focused you'll be after--

BEN: *(Tries to ignore her.)*

JO: Fine have it your way… I'll smoke by myself. *(JO lights her pipe and starts to smoke by herself in bed. BEN continues to write but now he is distracted. He gives up.)*

BEN: Allllllrighttttt. Gimme some.

JO: Here…

(The two pass the pipe back and forth for a couple minutes until they are really high … the lights go to instant blackout. Lights come back up quickly and we see the two on them sitting on the floor. They are high as kites. JO is laying with her head in BENS lap and BEN is resting against the bed.)

JO: Can you take a second and break it down for me so I can help you? We are collaborators if you can recall…

BEN: It's not ready yet…

JO: Fine.

BEN: It's good though.

JO: *(Mocking him)* You did a good job Benny.

BEN: Can I ask you something?

JO: Sure.

BEN: Why don't you have a boyfriend?

JO: Really? *(JO sits up so she can face BEN.)*

BEN: Yeah.

JO: Why?

BEN: I'm asking you.

JO: No. Why do you want to know why I don't have a boyfriend?

BEN: I just think it's weird.

JO: What?

BEN: The fact that you don't have a boyfriend.

JO: You are not being very clear my friend.

BEN: The weed makes my mind fuzzy.

JO: I don't know.

BEN: Don't know what?

JO: Why.

BEN: Why what?

JO: Does weed drastically drop your IQ as well?

BEN: Oh… why you don't have a boyfriend.

JO: I really don't understand it… I mean … I'm crazy … irrational… impulsive … kind of a mess. Those could be some contributing factors---

BEN: Yeah but it still doesn't make sense. *(PAUSE)* I think you're great. You're smart, funny, witty, talented, -- beautiful. I just wonder… how a girl who looks like you… has a BODY like you do… and a BRAIN… doesn't have a boyfriend. ---- You're awesome Jo.

JO: Why do I need a boyfriend when I have someone like you who fucks me AND says that kind of shit to me?

BEN: I'm not your boyfriend Jo.

JO: I've been acutely aware of that fact for quite some time now. *(PAUSE)* And since we're playing the personal question game… I have one for you.

BEN: Shoot.

JO: Why are you still in a long distance relationship?

BEN: I love my girlfriend.

JO: *(Laughing)* Do ya now?

BEN: Yeah, I really do.

JO: *(Not trying to egg him on but seriously asking)* Do you think about her when you're fucking me?

BEN: Jo! Come on…

JO: Well do you? You love her so much; I find it hard to believe you just forget about her when you're inside me.

BEN: You wouldn't understand.

JO: Well, I'm trying to. I don't completely understand our relationship. We have no idea what we're doing. You are so fucking lost and you don't know what to do about it. You're a lost boy Benny… a confused lost boy, who has NO idea what he wants.

BEN: *(exploding)* She's not here okay. I miss her! She's really awesome… and in some crazy fucked up world part of me thinks the two of you would actually be friends… but she's not here. And you too… you're so different… you're both beautiful… you're both sweet and kind … but … there is something… about you too… that has me just… torn the fuck up! And you're right there. I can see you without using Skype, I can hear you talk without a phone, I can see you every day if I wanted to without having to get on a plane. *(REALIZATION)* You're so much fun to hang out with… We get along so well…You are beautiful. Crazy beautiful, and we write some pretty great shit together. You're right. I don't know what I want because I want you when I'm around you. I want you so bad that I can't keep my hands off you. I know that's not right. I know that I shouldn't be cheating on my girlfriend… but I can't figure any of that out right now… It's so complicated Jo… THREE YEARS is a long time to be with someone. I know everything about her! I know what makes her mad, I know what makes her happy… I know NOTHING about you. I just know that you are here… right now… standing in front of me… and I need that.

JO: Oh… so I'm your filler girlfriend. Here when you need me because she can't be. Here for you to have so you don't have to spend a night alone. Here for your own pleasure. A girlfriend without the perks of being actually loved.

BEN: You're not my girlfriend at all.

JO: No, I am not.

(PAUSE)

16

(The BEN and JO start moving around the room trying to shake off that last conversation. JO may sit down and try to write. BEN may change into PJ's. Aimless movement to pass the time.)

BEN: We should find you a guy.

JO: *(almost losing it)* Are you kidding? Was that really just your segway out of that conversation?! Okay fine… only because… whatever… Yes please. My OKCupid mailbox is getting full with winners and I hardly have time to date them all.

BEN: I'm serious Jo! I bet we can find you a really great guy. I can be an awesome wingman. Think about it. Me and you go to a bar… we're having a few beers… the guys in the bar all think you're with me… so naturally they're jealous … and bummed that you're taken. Then I casually go over to a group of fine upstanding gentleman and drop hints to the guy you like the most. I'll say things like "yeah that's my great friend Jo… she's awesome… she likes baseball and she writes comedy." You know stuff like that. The guy will totally go over and talk to you… the rest, is basically a fairytale.

JO: Sounds like a solid plan Benny. Perhaps after this writers retreat we embark on a couples retreat. Except the idea behind it is to put me in a couple and help you manage your own.

BEN: I thought we weren't going to talk about my relationship anymore…

JO: I can't let it go… sorry I'm a girl, we harp on things longer than we should… but I hear how you and your girlfriend talk on the phone… I mean, I understand… you're in a long distance relationship… but … I mean … I don't really know what I'm talking about… I've never been in a relationship, let alone a long distance one… but it just seems so hard. Like … she's not done with school for another year right? That's 365 days. A bunch of fucking weeks… and 12 months. That's a long time. I don't know how you do it…. And then to not be just exploding with love when you talk on the phone? Or skype? I mean … after so much time has gone by shouldn't you be itching to talk to her? Wishing every moment of the day you could hold her? I'm starting to think I read too many Nicholas Sparks novels… I really am saying too much… *(PAUSE)* I mean you shouldn't want to be with me ya know? Like, I'm just now starting to realize how … fucked up all this is. You said you think in some crazy fucked up world I could be your girlfriend's FRIEND. That is insane to me… literally insane. You are crazy Ben… I mean I thought

I was crazy… but… you got some deep seeded issues man… and the worst part is… I still want you.

BEN: You may be right… I may be crazy.

JO: Really? Quoting Billy Joel at a time like this? You are a lunatic.

BEN: I just may be THE lunatic you're looking for.

JO: Ridiculous. You should probably date me. JUST A SUGGESTION. *(PAUSE)* Alright… I'm really tired.

(She goes to stand up. BEN grabs her and pulls her into his lap. He stares at her for a few moments.)

BEN: You really are amazing Jo.

(Before she can even respond he kisses her. BEN lifts JO up. He is carrying her. They go over to the bed, kissing the whole time. The lights start to fade as BEN slowly lowers him and JO onto the bed. LIGHTS OUT.)

SCENE 2

(Lights up on BEN and JO lying in bed. JO is lying on BEN's chest. They are cuddling. BEN wakes up first and notices the sleep situation. He relaxes into it. He kisses JO very softly on the forehead. JO stirs and BEN lets her roll into his arms. He is holding her and he never has before. He knows he won't ever get this moment again with JO, so he enjoys it. He falls back to sleep and as he does JO wakes up and notices where she is. JO couldn't be happier about the sleeping arrangement, but she scoots out from BEN'S arms and sits up in bed. She stares at BEN for a moment just enjoying the quiet moment. She grabs her laptop and tries to write.)

BEN: Good morning.

JO: Hello.

BEN: Whatcha doing?

JO: Trying to write.

BEN: And how's it going?

JO: What?

BEN: The writing.

JO: Not good.

BEN: Stuck?

JO: Very.

BEN: Write about something you know.

JO: Classic response.

BEN: Want to hear something I wrote?

JO: Please! You've never offered up any material before... this is awesome!

BEN: It's not a sketch or anything...

JO: Just read it...

BEN: Okay... (*BEN takes a minute. He knows there is no turning back after he reads this poem.*)

> Torn. Between You
> Torn. Between Her
> Broken. You are away
> Broken. She's right here
> Lying. To myself
> Lying. To you
> Lying. To her
> This hurts.
> This hurts.
> You are not here.
> She is asleep next to me.
> She doesn't know I'm writing this.
> You don't know I'm sleeping with her.
> She doesn't know how beautiful she is
> When she is asleep on my shoulder
> You don't know I think she's that beautiful.
> I don't know what it all means.
> I just know, that you are not here
> She is
> I am lost
> And someone is going to get hurt.

(*There is a ridiculously long pause as Jo lets that bomb register.*)

JO: When did you write that?

BEN: Last night.

JO: Why?

BEN: I don't know--

JO: Yes you do. You know. You don't just write a poem like that and not know why you did.

BEN: That was ... just ... such ... a huge step for me...

JO: Ben... what's going on?

BEN: I'm ... just really confused.

JO: I've been confused about you for months, that doesn't mean I go writing poems about it! I kept my feelings to myself… because I didn't want to lose you! This is too much to handle first thing in the morning.

BEN: I can't lose you Jo…

JO: Do you understand what you have done?

BEN: Yes.

JO: *(Hurt)* Good as long as we're clear. *(JO rushes into the bathroom and slams the door behind her. BEN stands in the room unsure of what to do next. He paces and paces, waiting for JO to reappear. He goes over to his work space and grabs a bunch of papers and starts reading. As he is reading he starts to rip up pages and throw them around the room. Jo quietly opens the door and watches BEN destroy his own words. BLACKOUT.)*

(When the lights comes back up it should appear that some time has passed. JO and BEN are sitting on opposite ends of the room. It's clear that the two haven't spoken in hours. JO is staring at her laptop and BEN has his head on a pile of papers he just ripped up.)

JO: Benny---

BEN: What?

JO: Did you know? That I felt… that way about you?

BEN: Not until… well no… kind of… I never knew what to believe really… then last night happened… and this whole weekend…

JO: I've always liked you… I tried to hide it from you. I didn't want to say something that made you run away. I wanted to stay your… whatever I am to you … for as long as I could. But this retreat… these three days… they've changed everything. ---- I used to be afraid to be honest with you. I used to think I had to keep a lid on my emotions but… but you changed that. You opened up the flood gates. You made it okay for me to tell you how I feel…*(PAUSE)* I am falling in love with you Benny. Since last night… when you called me beautiful and said all those things about me… my mind has been spinning… then you read that poem… and for the first time in a long time… I felt… SOMETHING. I felt like I am allowed to be loved back… and I felt it come from you… like this crazy force that I can't really describe. In less than 48 hours you have turned by world upside down and I have no idea how you did it or why it's affecting me like this… But something was burning inside me last night… I mean, I might have just been really high… but I don't think so… I think this is something… whether we want to admit it or not… this is something big.

BEN: Come here.

(*JO walks over to BEN and kisses him softly on the lips. He goes to put his arms around her but she gently pushes him to the bed. He sits. She stands in front of him and starts to unbutton her shirt.*)

JO: Write about this.

(*JO starts to undress and BEN watches her. The lights start to fade and BEN grabs JO and gently brings her to the bed. They lay down kissing each other slowly. BLACK OUT.*)

SCENE 3

(*Lights up on BEN sleeping in bed. JO is at his desk reading something on his laptop. She is dressed for a new day. Her duffle bag is packed and sitting by the door. She is ready to leave. She closes the laptop as BEN wakes up.*)

BEN: You're up early.

JO: It's 11am.

BEN: I forgot… you're used to working breakfast shifts---

JO: Damn my internal clock---

BEN: Whatcha doing over there?

JO: Reading.

BEN: Yeah?

JO: I figured out who the two people are you're writing about.

BEN: I wasn't trying to be discreet.

JO: It's really good…

BEN: Jo---

JO: What?

BEN: You read the ending?

JO: I did.

BEN: I'm sorry.

JO: Don't change it.

BEN: Why?

JO: That's how you want it to end… so that's how it's going to end.

BEN: It's just a story!

JO: This thing… that we have… it's done today.

BEN: Stop it---

JO: You leave her and stay with me … or nothing.

BEN: Jo---

JO: It's been a real eye opening three days Benny… I'll see you at work later.

BEN: Jo don't leave yet!

JO: *(Losing it)* I can't stay here Benny. I mean … I kind of thought you might come around this weekend. I thought you might actually consider being with me instead of a long distance relationship. But, had I known you already had the ending of this weekend mapped out perfectly in your story… perhaps I would have changed some of my dialogue and I wouldn't have wasted so much of my breath. Did you just ask me to come here so that you could write the story truthfully? Because there is a difference between based on a true story and a TRUE story. ----- I hope you know I'll be seeking royalties for this when it's published…

BEN: I didn't mean for all this to happen this weekend Jo. You told me to write that story…

JO: How could you not? Our story is cinematic gold. Boy meets girl. Girl is pretty with red hair and has a mouth like a truck driver but it doesn't matter because it's part of her charm. Boy is insanely handsome with skin the color of wheat and has an incredibly charming and sweet personality. Girl likes the boy instantly because they have so much in common and enjoy each other's company. Boy likes girl too but has a girlfriend. CONFLICT. Boy and girl go out to a bar one night with a bunch of co-workers. Boy starts flirting with girl who can't resist him. Boy kisses girl on a quiet street later that night and tells her she's beautiful and special. Boy invites girl back to his apartment and they begin a two month long fuck a thon, no strings attached. Girl starts feeling like shit but she doesn't want to lose Boy because Boy makes her happy, but she can't really get over the fact that this relationship will never be anything more than a physical one. Boy starts to drown in his own deception because he's hurting two people and fucking himself over. Boy and Girl go on a writers retreat to write a script for a producer who wants to work with them. INSERT PAST THREE DAYS HERE… Boy decides in the shadows of the night, while Girl is asleep, that he is going to stay with his girlfriend. Girl wakes up and finds that out. Girl is destroyed. *(LONG PAUSE)* I don't think Nora Ephron or Stephanie Meyer could have conjured up such tragic romantic perfection.

BEN: Listen Jo… you knew the score… You knew from the beginning that I had a girlfriend… you knew we have been together for four years… I'm sorry that you woke up and read that… I was going to talk to you… and … Jo this… wasn't easy for me… You're not the only one who feels like shit… but I had to figure it out… I had to make a decision---

JO: THIS ISN'T THE BACHELOR BEN… YOU DON'T GET TO PASS OUT ROSES TO THE WOMAN YOU CHOSE AT THE END AND THEN RUNAWAY TOGETHER IN A HELICOPTER PAID FOR BY ABC STUDIOS!

BEN: Stop yelling! ---- I left something out of the end of the story… because I knew you were going to get a hold of my laptop at some point this weekend… and I knew you were going to read that---

JO: What did you forget to write? You and your girlfriend living happy ever after? Because it's implied---

BEN: She's moving to the city at the end of the month.

(BOOM. The bomb has been dropped and it takes everything in JO's body to not collapse. Or kill BEN.)

JO: You knew this whole time… You knew… for how long… that she was moving here?

BEN: For a month now… She just got transferred to another program here in the city…

JO: *(Overwhelmed)*: A month?! You knew for a month … that she was … and you didn't… oh my god… you just … with me? How could you? Benny… after everything? *(JO sits on the bed; she can't hold herself up anymore.)* You are NOT the person I thought you were. I mean… I had my doubts about your moral compass from the second you said you had a girlfriend, but you still wanted to see me… but I still thought you were a good guy. Like, I thought you were a REALLY good guy. *(JO is saying all this to BEN but she isn't facing him. She doesn't want to look at him.)* I figured you were just lost… trying to figure shit out… I thought I could handle being the other woman… but fuck; I'm not equipped for this… I can't handle this… because I don't know how to be the other woman… you're not supposed to fall in love with the man who has a girlfriend… RULE NUMBER ONE… *(PAUSE. Starting to gain back her composure. She does not want to seem weak in this moment.)* I am leaving. I understand we work together, don't worry… I won't make it weird… I won't make the restaurant a hostile work environment. I'm good at pretending in public. As for our writing partnership… that's going to be a tough one. I can pretend in public… but if you get me behind closed doors and just act like nothing between us ever happened… which you will … I won't be able to handle it. It will hurt me more than anything… because you and I will both know that what we're doing is stupid and hurtful, for both of us. *(JO turns to look BEN right in the eye.)* So … this story… was the last one we write together. *(JO gets up and grabs her duffle bag. She goes to the door. She waits with her hand on the door knob for a second, hoping Ben will stop her. He doesn't. He sits in bed and watches her go. She turns the knob and walks out the door. BEN sits there for a few minutes. He grabs his laptop and starts reading the story. He is going through a silent range of emotions. BEN gets up and goes to the door to go after JO but then he reconsiders. Instead, he reaches into his backpack, grabs his phone, and dials.)*

BEN: *(on the phone)* Hey baby… I miss you too…
(BLACKOUT)

END OF PLAY

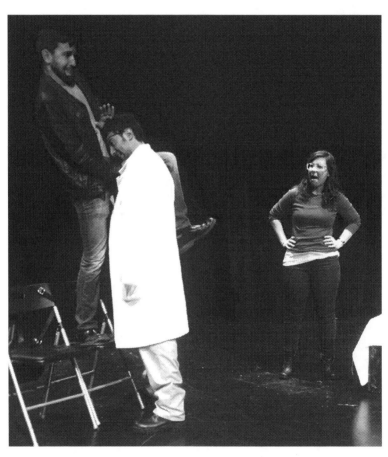

David Vega *as TONY,* Freddy Valle *as DUMAS,*
Michelle Berenice Brino *as ALLISON*
in A SONG A DAY KEEPS THE DOCTOR AWAY by Freddy Valle.

A Song A Day Keeps The Doctor Away

By Freddy Valle

Freddy Valle is an actor and playwright based in Miami, Florida. He is a graduate from New World School of the Arts (BFA). He has performed for several companies in South Florida including: Outre Theatre, Micro Theatre Miami and Miami Stage Company. As a playwright, Freddy has had his plays produced at Micro Theatre Miami, The Strawberry One-Act Festival in NYC, and the Ft. Lauderdale Fringe Festival.

A Song A Day Keeps The Doctor Away made its New York City debut on February 14, 2015 at The Hudson Guild Theatre. It was one of the finalists in The Riant Theatre's Winter 2015 Strawberry One-Act Festival with the following cast:

TONY	David Vega
ALLISON	Michelle Berenice Brino
DUMAS	Freddy Valle

The play was directed by Tatyana-Marie Carlo

CAST OF CHARACTERS

TONY, a man in his 20's with a peculiar medical problem. Instead of speaking, he sings all of his lines. He is worried it could be fatal.

ALLISON, Tony's girlfriend, also in her 20's. She is very energetic, passionate and intense.

DUMAS, 20's. A young aspiring doctor. He has an eye patch and a missing arm. He is eager and optimistic.

SCENE 1

(We see ALLISON and TONY in a doctor's examination room. TONY sits on the examination. ALLISON is seated in a chair near the examination table. She anxiously keeps checking her watch for the time.)

ALLISON: Uh… How much longer can they take? It's not like they have a dying patient or anything. How are you feeling honey? *(TONY Barely opens his mouth to speak, but ALLISON cuts him off. Throughout the following monologue, TONY attempts to interject but cannot find a proper spot to speak. ALLISON tramples over his lines.)* I knew it, I knew it had gotten worse. What are we going to do? Crap. Crap crap crap. I don't know what we're going to tell your mom. What will people say? I can't date someone in your condition. I should have listened to Michelle. She said it wouldn't last, but no I had hope, and expectations. But now we're doomed, forever doomed. Okay maybe I'm being a bit dramatic, but I've never dated anyone in your situation. I know what you're going to say: 'Oh baby please, it's fine, I promise this never happens'. It wouldn't be the first time I've heard that. You wouldn't believe the excuses men come up with. What am I saying? You know what? We will overcome this. We're strong. You're strong. And who am I to judge right? …Why are you so quiet? You're scaring me! Say something! Talk! *(Just as TONY is about to finally respond, DUMAS enters. He is wearing an eye patch and is missing his left arm. There is only a little stump of an arm left.)* Hello Doctor— wait, you're not Doctor Wilson.

DUMAS: Doctor Wilson is currently on vacation. So I'll be filling in.

ALLISON: Are you sure you're the appropriate individual for this job?

DUMAS: What does that mean?

ALLISON: My boyfriend Tony here, has a very challenging condition. And I want to be sure that you are the correct person for the task at hand.

DUMAS: Are you asking if I'm qualified?

ALLISON: Maybe… Yes.

DUMAS: Rest assured I am more than qualified. You'd be surprised how often people ask me that. I know, I have a young face. But looks can be deceiving.

ALLISON: Yes… looks.

DUMAS: So, Tony right? What seems to be the problem? *(TONY attempts to speak, but is interrupted.)*

ALLISON: You're missing an arm.

DUMAS: Excuse me?

ALLISON: And you have an eye patch.

DUMAS: Well—

ALLISON: Are you sure you're meant to be a doctor? I feel like the universe is trying to tell you something here.

DUMAS: It's not like I need both arms and eyes to be in this profession.

ALLISON: You kind of do. What about depth perception? What if you stick the needle in the wrong vein? You could seriously hurt someone. And what if—

DUMAS: Miss, I assure you I am more than capable of doing this job. Now, we need to attend to the health of Mr. Tony here, alright?

ALLISON: Alright. I'm just worried is all.

DUMAS: Yes. I understand.

ALLISON: Because Doctor Wilson is his doctor.

DUMAS: I understand.

ALLISON: Yes.

DUMAS: Yes.

ALLISON: Okay.

DUMAS: Okay.

ALLISON: Great.

DUMAS: Great. So Tony, what seems to be the problem? *(TONY motions to answer but is interrupted again.)*

ALLISON: I'm sorry, what was your name again?

DUMAS: Miss, I'm trying to treat Tony.

ALLISON: Yes, but I need to know you're name in case we have to sue for malpractice or something.

DUMAS: My name is Albert Dumas. Can I treat Tony now?

ALLISON: Wait wait, Dumas? Is that a fancy way of saying—

DUMAS: No no no no. It's Dumas. Dumas. Just Dumas.

ALLISON: Are you sure? Because that sounds an awful lot like—

DUMAS: Yes I know, but it's French, Dumas. Miss, I need to tend to Tony!

ALLISON: Yes Doctor Dumas, because he has a very serious ailment. And I am sure Dumas can handle it.

DUMAS: So Tony? What is the problem?

(All of TONY's lines are sung in an operatic fashion unless indicated otherwise.)

TONY: Doctor, I can't talk properly anymore. Every time I speak I end up singing. As you can imagine it's severely affected my day to day living. I am very scared of what this could mean.

DUMAS: What? This is outrageous. How is this even possible?

ALLISON: You think that's crazy? You should hear the sex.

TONY: Allison this is no joke. I can't stop, I'm really concerned. What if it's something serious?

DUMAS: It could be something neurological, something that's impeding with your brain's ability to properly communicate. This is amazing, I've never heard of anything like this.

ALLISON: So if it's in his brain, does that— Oh my god, he has a tumor or something. He has cancer doesn't he? Its terminal isn't it? I knew it.

TONY: There's a moment you know you're fucked!

ALLISON: I couldn't have put it better myself baby.

TONY: Not an inch more room to self destruct.

DUMAS: Will everyone be quiet for a second? I never said cancer! I was only speculating, analyzing the situation. It could be anything really.

ALLISON: So it could be cancer then.

TONY: Yeah you're fucked alright! And all for spite—

DUMAS: It's not cancer! So everyone please calm down. Tony, please have a seat for me. Alright, Tony please say 'ah' for me. *(TONY sings 'ah' and sustains it. DUMAS starts to look down his throat and then smells TONY's breathe.)* You're throat seems fine. *(DUMAS grabs TONY's wrist and listens to his pulse.)* Your pulse is normal. *(DUMAS takes TONY's temperature by placing his stump arm on TONY's forehead.)* And no fever, how odd.

ALLISON: Excuse me, how come you're not using any of your doctor tools? Where's your stethamascope? Tongue oppressor? Mouth flashlight? Ear stick?

TONY: Yes, your lack of tools worries me.

DUMAS: I, um, didn't have time to grab them, yes. Because I heard Tony needed urgent and immediate care and so I rushed here as quickly as I could.

ALLISON: We were waiting here for thirty minutes.

TONY: There is something fishy going on here.

DUMAS: I find your lack of faith disturbing.

ALLISON: I find your lack of tools even more disturbing. You're really living up to your name right now Dumas.

TONY: Dumas you're a dumbass!

ALLISON: Yeah you tell him baby! Dumbass!

DUMAS: I don't appreciate the hostility right now.

ALLISON: You're a big effin' dumbass!

DUMAS: You guys are totally hurting my feelings.

TONY: I'm the one with the singing problem.

ALLISON: Yeah!

TONY: What about my feelings?

ALLISON: His feelings?

DUMAS: You sing beautifully if you ask me.

ALLISON: Hell yeah!

TONY: Try ordering food.

ALLISON: Ordering food.

TONY: It's very embarrassing.

ALLISON: So embarrassing.

TONY: I need a solution right now.

ALLISON: Right now!

TONY: And frankly both of you—

ALLISON: Both of us.

TONY: Are starting to annoy me!

ALLISON: Are starting to annoy—wait what? I'm annoying you? I don't see how I could possibly be annoying you. I am like the most considerate and loving person ever.

(While ALLISON is speaking, DUMAS approaches TONY. He then stomps on TONY's foot testing his reflexes.)

TONY: Ow! That really hurt. You know, I'm starting to doubt you're an actual doctor. Who are you? Who who? Who who?

DUMAS: I love that song!

TONY: *(TONY aggressively grabs DUMAS by his coat.)* WHO ARE YOU?! WHO ARE YOU?!

DUMAS: Aaaah! Okay okay okay, I'm not a real doctor.

ALLISON: I knew it! Ha! I bet that arm and eye patch are fake too.

(She tries to look under DUMAS' eye patch, but realizes that it's real.)

DUMAS: No, those are real. I'm sorry, it's just that the doctor is out and I've always wanted to be a doctor. I'm his assistant. And sure, I may not have much experience, but please please let me try solving this. I know I can do it if you give me a shot. Please? I've watched more than enough of *House* and *Grey's Anatomy* so I can do this. And that has to count for something no? Come on. Please?

ALLISON: Tony would never give in to your pathetic attempt to play doctor. *(She gathers herself and her belongings and motions TONY to leave. However, TONY considers the proposition.)*

TONY: Alright I'll do it, but only because I desperately need this singing to go away.

DUMAS: Yes! Thank you thank you thank you. So obviously this isn't a typical ailment, so I'm sure we'll need atypical treatment. I've got it, try holding your breathe for ten seconds.

ALLISON: How's that going to work?

DUMAS: It's worth a shot. Do it.

(TONY holds his breathe for ten seconds. ALLISON stares intently. DUMAS starts counting with his fingers. Once he reaches five, he nudges TONY to finish the last five counts. TONY then exhales audibly.)

TONY: Let's see if it worked. *(TONY now sings in the style of Shakira. The actor playing TONY embodies the artist, physically and vocally. Therefore, a lot of belly dancing and hip movements.)* Baby! Ay Ay Ay! Oh no, it's turned into something else.

ALLISON: You're killing it baby!

TONY: This isn't funny. I don't want to do this anymore. *(Vigorously shakes hips.)*

ALLISON: Look at those hips.

DUMAS: At least it's progress. Let's scare it out of him.

ALLISON: Are we treating the singing or the hiccups?

DUMAS: Just do it. Let's see, are you afraid of the dark?

(DUMAS turns off the lights. In the darkness we hear poor attempts at spooky sounds from both ALLISON and DUMAS. After a few moments, ALLISON turns the lights back on. We then see DUMAS and TONY in a compromising position, unaware to the fact that the lights came on. ALLISON stares for a brief moment. DUMAS then realizes the lights have returned, and quickly composes himself.)

ALLISON: This isn't working. I have a better idea. Tony... I cheated on you with your best friend.

TONY: What?

DUMAS: He didn't sing that. You did it.

(TONY sings again in the style of Michael Jackson. Again, embodying the artist. Pelvic thrusts, groin grabs, moon walks, etc.)

TONY: How can you break my heart like that baby. You're bad, you're bad, I knew it all along. Hee hee!

ALLISON: You should really try out for American Idol or America's Got Talent because you are too good.

TONY: Jamona! No, I won't ever do what you want me to do. It's over, *(Sadly.)* hee hee.

ALLISON: Baby, I was kidding, I just wanted to scare you. I would never cheat on you.

DUMAS: *(In a melodramatic soup opera fashion.)* TONY YOU HAVE CANCER!

ALLISON: *(Joining, catching on to DUMAS' tactic.)* I THOUGHT YOU SAID HE DIDN'T HAVE CANCER.

DUMAS: HE HAS THE CANCER! TONY YOU'RE GOING TO DIE!

(ALLISON and DUMAS fall to their knees in an over-the-top fashion. Groaning and moaning, mourning TONY and his "cancer".)

TONY: Nuh-uh, that ain't gonna work on me anymore, I don't have cancer. So just beat it!

(DUMAS slaps TONY across the face.)

ALLISON: What the hell is your problem?

DUMAS: He said beat it. There was fire in his eyes. And his words were pretty clear. He said beat it.

ALLISON: You think you're clever? You just assaulted my boyfriend.

(TONY recovers, this time he is singing in Spanish in a mariachi fashion.)

TONY: Me dolio tanto. Porque me distes tan duro? Yo voy a llorar. Llorar y llorar. Llorar y llorar.

DUMAS: Si. Tu biblioteca es in carro. Nosotros, vosotros ir para azul.

TONY: Que? De que me estas hablando idiota?

DUMAS: Tu tenny much mucho DeNiro in su trucky-trailer?

ALLISON: You speak Spanish?

DUMAS: Yeah I minored in it.

ALLISON: Slap him again.

(DUMAS slaps TONY again. TONY is now rapping in English.)

TONY: Will you stop hitting me! It really hurts. I'm gonna pound you, and unsound you, till I've unwound you and the inner workings of this fake. Who puts other's lives at stake. I can't concentrate. I despise the unwise who imitate the pros. Under your guise of lies I was taking your blows. But no moh. I'm sick of this ish. Ima scratch you like a punk itch. Prepare to taste my fist. Bitch.

ALLISON: Dammnit Tony! Get better! You're frustrating me.

TONY: Man, bitches be cray.

ALLISON: Oh yeah? Yeah? Well you be more cray, dawg. Oh screw this.

(ALLISON grabs DUMAS and kisses him and starts making out with him. TONY is astounded. DUMAS is dumbfounded. TONY responds in his regular voice.)

TONY: Allison Marie Hartman, how dare you make out with my fake doctor in front of me? I am your boyfriend. He's a dumbass. Literally, his name is dumbass. I have been nothing but faithful and loving and caring. The least you could do is have the decency to cheat behind my back!

ALLISON: Baby, you're talking. You can talk again!

TONY: I'm talking, I'm not singing. I'm back.

ALLISON: You're back.

TONY: I'm back!

(ALLISON kisses TONY. During TONY's rant, DUMAS managed to hide underneath the examination table. He now emerges, unharmed.)

DUMAS: What happened?

TONY: I don't know. I just got so mad, and I wanted to hurt you really really badly. It was a rush, but I don't know, somehow it worked. Dumas, thank you. I guess you're not such a Dumas afterall.

DUMAS: Thanks.

TONY: Babe, let's go out. Let's have dinner. And let's just talk about our feelings.

ALLISON: Yes yes yes. I'm so happy to have you back to normal. Well thank you Mister Dumas.

DUMAS: Doctor Dumas.

ALLISON: Really?

TONY: Ha!

DUMAS: You don't—

ALLISON: Not really.

DUMAS: I mean—

TONY: Seriously?

DUMAS: Well—

ALLISON: Meh?

DUMAS: Yeah you're right.

ALLISON: Have a nice day.

TONY: Yes, again thank you. Goodbye.

(TONY and ALLISON gather their belongings, and begin to exit.)

DUMAS: Yes goodbye. You say goodbye, but I say hello. Hello hello, I don't know why you say goodbye I say hello.

(DUMAS realizes what has just occurred. ALLISON and TONY slowly turn back and look at him. DUMAS tries to speak again, but now he is singing.)

DUMAS: Help! I need somebody. Help! Not just anybody. Help! You know I need someone. HEELLLPP!

(Blackout.)

The End

WHERE'S THE REST OF ME? by David E. Tolchinsky.

Where's the Rest of Me?

By David E. Tolchinsky

David E. Tolchinsky is the founder/director of Northwestern University's MFA in Writing for Screen+Stage program. As a screenwriter, he has been commissioned by multiple companies to write screenplays, and his feature *Girl* is distributed by Sony. He was ranked 14th on New City's *Film 50: Chicago's Screen Gems 2013* and was the recipient of a 2014 Illinois Arts Council Artist Fellowship in Literature (Poetry, Prose, Scriptworks). He is a graduate of Yale (BA) and USC School of Cinematic Arts (MFA). *Where's the Rest of Me?* marked his debut as a playwright and theatre director. More information at davidetolchinsky.com.

Where's the Rest of Me? premiered on February 14, 2015, at the Hudson Guild Theatre, New York City. It was nominated for Best Play in the 2015 Strawberry One-Act Play Festival with the following cast in the order of appearance:

SPALDING GRAY	Evan Brenner
DAVE	Greg Peace
ALL OTHER CHARACTERS	Camara McLaughlin
MARSHALL EDELSON	Armand Eisen

Greg Peace was nominated for Best Actor and Camara McLaughlin was nominated for Best Actress for their performances.

The play was directed by the playwright, David E. Tolchinsky, who won the award for Best Director of the festival. Other crew included: Jessy Lynn (producer), Lila Rachel Becker (assistant director), Kelley Sener (production manager), Erika Degraffinreaidt (costume designer), Rob Lees (poster design), and Jingyang Cheng (videographer), who was nominated for Best Trailer/Video Diary.

CAST OF CHARACTERS

DAVE, 40s, an aging hipster, ironic Clark Kent glasses and Converse.

SPALDING GRAY, 55, a monologist, prematurely gray, plaid shirt, understated Maine demeanor.

MARSHALL EDELSON, 60s, an academic psychiatrist, bushy eyebrows, unironic Clark Kent glasses, sweater, unironic pens in a pocket penholder. He's Dave's father.

A range of characters all played by THE SAME ACTRESS:
> AN AIRLINE REPRESENTATIVE
> AN AIRLINE GUARD
> DAVE'S HIGH SCHOOL GIRLFRIEND
> DEBRA, DAVE'S WIFE
> RONALD REAGAN
> PARRIS FROM THE MOVIE *KING'S ROW*
> THE SURGEON FROM *KING'S ROW*
> THE SURGEON'S DAUGHTER FROM *KING'S ROW*
> VARIOUS HIPSTER RESIDENCY PARTICIPANTS
> A MAKEOVER TV PRODUCER
> A DOCTOR
> MAYBE A DOG

SETTINGS

Spalding Gray's room. A desk, a chair. A light.

Marshall Edelson's room. A chair. Cabinets of DVDs and various TVs, all showing home movies and classic movies, including *King's Row*.

A bare stage, perhaps with props — a bicycle, a telephone, etc. — and perhaps with a large rear-projection movie screen.

TIME

The Present.

PRODUCTION NOTES

Spalding Gray and Marshall Edelson each have their own rooms. These rooms may be on different parts of the stage, or perhaps these rooms exist in different parts of a gallery or theatre or house and Dave walks from one room to the other as the audience follows.

You might make use of a screen to visualize scenes from *King's Row*, Dave's life, or whatever. Or this might be accomplished in a more abstract way.

The actor playing the various characters might utilize masks, images on the screen, or just a different affect and place on the stage to make the transformation.

There's a dog at the end of the play. Whether a prop, an actress in a dog mask, a puppet, or an actual dog, it should feel poetically threatening.

Depending on how you actualize the dog, you may choose to have Dave speak this line to clarify and emphasize the action: *He came towards me. And I held out my hand and he . . . did nothing and he ran back to his house.*

CURTAIN UP

(DAVE, a good-looking, aging hipster with the requisite shaved head and big black Clark Kent glasses, walks onto stage and addresses the audience.)
DAVE: In 2001, I was invited to participate in a three-week artists' residency in New Smyrna Beach, Florida, directed by Spalding Gray. *(Lights up on the Spalding Gray room. SPALDING, in his plaid shirt, sits at his desk.)*
DAVE: Spalding Gray, who invented the full-length monologue, usually autobiographical, mostly humorous, and delivered while sitting on a bare stage in front of a spare desk. He was supposedly going to teach ten of us mid-career writers and performers chosen from around the globe to do what he did. Create monologues, that is. But Spalding Gray wasn't there when we arrived.
(SPALDING gets up from the desk and walks towards the front of the stage. The AIRLINE REPRESENTATIVE appears.)
AIRLINE REPRESENTATIVE: Now boarding Group 2.
SPALDING *(coming up to her)*: This plane is going to explode.

AIRLINE REPRESENTATIVE: You can't say that, sir.

SPALDING: Why not, this plane is going to explode.

(The REPRESENTATIVE becomes the GUARD.)

GUARD: You can't say that, sir —

SPALDING: Why not? This plane really is going to explode.

GUARD: If you say it one more time we're going to arrest you.

SPALDING: So arrest me, because this plane is going to fucking explode.

(The GUARD handcuffs him and leads him struggling off stage.)

DAVE: And we were all filled with anxiety: would Spalding somehow get out of jail or were we going to be forced to teach ourselves how to create and deliver full-length autobiographical monologues? In retrospect, the stakes didn't seem very high. / And part of me was relieved that Spalding Gray was in jail, because I didn't really want to learn how to deliver monologues and why was I in New Smyrna Beach anyway? / I was a screenwriter for God's sake, not a monologist.

(Perhaps a screen shows iconic images of a Hollywood screenwriter's life — cars, swimming pools, the Hollywood sign.)

DAVE: And sure, we screenwriters are often embarrassed and humiliated, but usually don't have to sit on a stage in front of an audience baring our autobiographical souls, as Spalding Gray did in each one of his performances. / And while I was waiting for Spalding Gray to arrive, for some reason, I started thinking about the movie *King's Row*.

(Lights up on the Edelson room, where MARSHALL, in his academic sweater, sits surrounded by books, DVDs, and various TVs showing classic movies, including King's Row.*)*

DAVE: My entire life my father would tell me —

MARSHALL *(looking anywhere but at DAVE)*: *King's Row* is the greatest movie ever made, David.

DAVE: As an aside, my father never made eye contact. *(to MARSHALL)* Greater than *The Bicycle Thief, City Lights, The Godfather, Casablanca,* or *Raging Bull,* Dad?

MARSHALL: Yes, David.

DAVE: He also rarely held my hand. *(to MARSHALL)* Greater than *Citizen Kane,* Dad?

MARSHALL: Yes, David. Trust me: *King's Row* is the greatest movie ever made.

(DAVE just looks at him, incredulous . . . and then . . .)

DAVE: It concerns a character named Parris (played by Robert Cummings) who lives in a small town named King's Row. Parris has a friend named Drake, played by Ronald Reagan.

(The GUARD becomes RONALD REAGAN.)

DAVE: Coincidentally, Ronald Reagan had been my grandmother's dance partner at a fundraiser.

(Cue Sinatra-esque dance music . . .)

DAVE: While they were dancing close, he said with great bitterness, according to my grandmother —

RONALD REAGAN: *King's Row* . . . It was my only good role.

DAVE: Which made me kinda like Ronald Reagan and made me wonder if my father was right. As to the plot: Parris plans to go to Vienna to practice psychiatry. What he soon realizes: there's enough mental illness right there in his own little town, so he stays. My father explained:

MARSHALL: This movie was the reason I became a psychiatrist, David. Shall we watch it again?

DAVE: I was six. *(to MARSHALL)* How about you teach me how to throw a ball instead, Dad?

MARSHALL: You know I can't do things like that.

DAVE: Why not, Dad?

MARSHALL: I have a very bad heart.

DAVE: Growing up, he would say this to me so often I remember it as a kind of daily prayer.

(MARSHALL moves to different areas of the stage as —)

DAVE: Can you teach me how to ride a bike, Dad?

MARSHALL: I have a bad heart, David. You know that.

DAVE: Can you help me build a tree house?

MARSHALL: My heart is bad, David.

DAVE: Well, how about a walk? Just a walk?

MARSHALL: David, you know I have a very bad heart.

DAVE: Dad —

MARSHALL: It's time you start realizing: I might be dead very soon, David, because of my very, very bad heart.

(DAVE just stares at him, disturbed.)

DAVE: Later in the movie, Drake falls off a train but is actually fine. However, the surgeon, the father of Drake's ex-girlfriend, announces:

(RONALD REAGAN becomes the SURGEON.)

SURGEON: The train hit Drake, his legs were crushed, they have to come off.

DAVE: The surgeon's daughter knows the operation is unnecessary but she's too late . . .

(The SURGEON saws off his legs.)

DAVE: Drake wakes up and he looks down to where his legs should be. And he yells to his spouse:

(The SURGEON becomes RONALD REAGAN.)

RONALD REAGAN: WHERE'S THE REST OF ME?! WHERE'S THE REST OF ME!?

DAVE: At age six, I pretended I couldn't walk.

(DAVE is on his knees.)

DAVE: My father had no idea I was pretending or what may have inspired me and thought I must have some kind of horrible undiagnosed ailment.

MARSHALL *(into the phone, reading from a medical textbook):* We need to rule out amyotrophic lateral sclerosis, Bell's palsy, systemic neuropathy, multiple sclerosis, sudden onset of rheumatoid arthritis, exposure to botulinum toxin, and venom from a Costa Rican eyelash viper snake. *(Beat)* No, he hasn't been to Costa Rica but he's not walking! God knows what's going on.

(Perhaps a screen shows RONALD REAGAN in King's Row.*)*

MARSHALL *(Beat):* Yes, we'll bring him in right away.

(MARSHALL gets off the phone.)

DAVE: So you're going to take me to the doctor, Dad?

MARSHALL: Your mother will take you.

DAVE: Why not you, Dad?

MARSHALL: David, I can't go to a doctor's office where there might be sick people in the waiting room, given my frail condition —

DAVE: Please?

(DAVE reaches for him.)

MARSHALL: David, your mother will take you and the doctor will figure out what's going on. I just hope it's not contagious.

(MARSHALL walks away. RONALD REAGAN becomes the DOCTOR.)

DOCTOR: He's fine. He's just looking for attention.

DAVE: That night —

MARSHALL: You can have a Fudgsicle, David, if you start walking.

(Marshall hold out a Fudgsicle. David . . . takes it bitterly and stands up.)

DAVE: And I started walking and we never spoke of it again. / Besides having a bad heart, my father was terrified of dogs.
(On a screen or on stage: A cute little dog.)

DAVE: He would see the neighborhood dog coming towards us wagging its tail, and would yell to me:

MARSHALL: DAVID, GET IN THE HOUSE NOW!
(DAVE anxiously runs towards MARSHALL and away from the dog.)

DAVE: Besides dogs, my father was also terrified of
(Perhaps on a screen: funny images fly by.)

DAVE: Children, police, bacteria, teachers, maids, cats, raccoons, packed-up boxes, insects, homosexuals, sunlight, marijuana, phone solicitors, flowers, public bathrooms, all my friends, and state borders. Not surprisingly, he had trouble sleeping.
(MARSHALL stands up and wanders up and down the stage, up and down stairs, into the audience and back again.)

DAVE: And I — well, I was now 16 . . .
(The DOCTOR becomes a GIRL, a girl DAVE likes, his first girlfriend. She and DAVE share some whiskey and a . . . first kiss. She walks off stage. DAVE is smiling ear to ear, excited until —)

MARSHALL: Where did you go tonight, David?

DAVE: Nowhere in particular. Well, goodnight, Dad —

MARSHALL *(following):* Who did you see tonight, David?

DAVE: No one in particular, just friends —

MARSHALL: Well, what did you do exactly? Where were you?

DAVE: Just out, Dad. With friends.

MARSHALL: Well, why are you so late?

DAVE: I'm tired, Dad. I'll see you in the morning.
(MARSHALL starts to say something, but DAVE walks off. / MARSHALL wanders, wanders, wanders as DAVE turns to watch him.)

DAVE: Now back in New Smyrna Beach, I talked to my spouse on the phone —
(DAVE's GIRLFRIEND becomes DEBRA, DAVE's spouse.)

DEBRA *(into a phone):* Dave, you left me alone with our two young kids for three weeks to hang out with Spalding Gray and he's not even there because he was too afraid to get on a plane?

DAVE *(into a phone):* He'll be here, Deb.

DEBRA: Why do you want to learn how to deliver monologues anyway, Dave? You're a screenwriter.

DAVE: Yeah I know I'm a screenwriter, and while I'm here I'm also working on a screenplay —

DEBRA: Maybe it's a way to look at things in your life, Dave, that you've avoided looking at?

DAVE: What are you talking about? It's just an opportunity to hang out with Spalding Gray, learn about monologues, and mostly I'm just working on my screenplay, OK?

DEBRA: Whatever you say, Dave. But you've been working on that screenplay awhile. I thought this was the year you were going to stop writing and start raising money to direct your feature.

DAVE: If Spalding doesn't show up soon, I'll fly home. OK? / Now back in *King's Row*, Drake is lying in bed, bitter and angry. He's not able to talk to his wife anymore and doesn't seem to care that his marriage is falling apart.

(SPALDING walks on stage . . .)

DAVE: So eventually Spalding Gray agreed not to talk about planes exploding anymore and they let him out of prison and somehow he built up enough courage to get on a plane to New Smyrna Beach.

(Spotlight on MARSHALL.)

DAVE: My father never built up enough courage to get on a plane to come to my wedding.

MARSHALL: I can't fly because of my heart, David.

DAVE *(to MARSHALL):* It's not your heart. It's your anxiety, Dad.

MARSHALL: You don't understand, David. My heart could fail at any minute and I'd be up in the plane and I'd die and is that what you want, David?

(DAVE has no answer.)

DAVE: And when Spalding arrived, he was immediately in crisis.

(SPALDING paces up and down the stage and into the audience somewhat like MARSHALL.)

SPALDING: The landscape is too flat. Where should I sit. What should I eat. Why did I come here. I never should have agreed to come here.

DAVE: And then, finally he settled down enough to conduct our first class. He told us how he constructed monologues:

SPALDING *(still pacing)*: I talk to my therapist about an upsetting series of events in my life.

DAVE: Like being arrested at the airport.

SPALDING: I see which parts my therapist laughs at. I throw out the rest, and slowly the piece takes shape. Each time I deliver the monologue, it becomes less a script and more a part of me until eventually I don't have to refer to notes at all. And I don't rehearse at all; I just listen to my old performances on tape.

(SPALDING sits at his desk.)

SPALDING: I imagine myself in the room delivering the monologue again, and always, even if the structure of the piece is loose and meandering, the ending makes it all work. The ending is what gives closure to the monologue and to the upsetting episode in my life. The ending tells me I have not just regurgitated my therapy sessions, but I have created something organic and whole.

(Spotlight on MARSHALL.)

DAVE: My father kept every window in our house closed. He kept all the shades down. If you opened a shade or a window, my father would shut it within minutes. He kept all the doors to the outside dead-bolted even though it was against fire regulations. One day, he replaced the turn locks on every window in the house with key locks that were always engaged. His home office was also always kept locked, supposedly because he kept patient records in there. But even after he stopped seeing patients and the room was used as a home theatre, it was still kept locked.

(Perhaps on a screen: pictures of MARSHALL's video collection)

DAVE: As videos and DVDs were released, he slowly collected over 7,000, including *King's Row* of course. / He had cabinet after cabinet built for his growing collection of movies. Each cabinet was kept locked. / As far as I know, my mother —

(DEBRA becomes DAVE'S MOTHER —)

DAVE: Didn't have keys to the cabinets holding the videos and DVDs. She didn't have keys to his office. She didn't have keys to the window locks. *(to MARSHALL)* Aren't you worried Mom could die in a fire?

MARSHALL: David, there are greater things to fear in life than fire.

(MARSHALL looks . . . And sees the small dog. Marshall backs away terrified, as does DAVE.)

DAVE: Meanwhile, my mother slowly developed chronic severe pain, dizziness, and crippling muscle cramps.

(DAVE'S MOTHER hunches over in pain.)

DAVE: Eventually they said it was lupus, although they couldn't be sure. Meanwhile, after years and years of dying, my father was still alive.
(MARSHALL watches DAVE'S MOTHER for a moment and then turns back to watching movies.)

DAVE: Back in New Smyrna Beach, we had a strenuous morning delivering our attempts at monologues that made Spalding pace faster and faster.
(Indeed, SPALDING gets up and paces as DAVE'S MOTHER becomes various RESIDENCY PARTICIPANTS.)

HIPSTER RESIDENCY PARTICIPANT 1: When I was 33, I had an affair with my wife's best friend. And my wife left me and now I'm all alone.

HIPSTER RESIDENCY PARTICIPANT 2: Let me tell you about the greatest story ever told. It stars a young carpenter named Jesus Christ —

HIPSTER RESIDENCY PARTICIPANT 3: When I was 60, I had sex for the first time.

HIPSTER RESIDENCY PARTICIPANT 4: When I was 16, I was gang raped at a party.

HIPSTER RESIDENCY PARTICIPANT 5: So the funniest thing happened to me when I was a kid: My dad hit me so hard my rib snapped. Well, maybe it wasn't that funny. But it was funnier than what he had done to my mother.

HIPSTER RESIDENCY PARTICIPANT 6: I used to be a drug addict. I don't know what was worst: licking the lining of my own pockets looking for drugs. Or watching my friends die one by one by one.
(SPALDING paces faster.)

DAVE: Listening to my colleagues bare their autobiographical souls, aware that Spalding was wishing he were anywhere else, my mind wandered.

MARSHALL: There are greater things to fear in life than fire.
(One of the PARTICIPANTS becomes RONALD REAGAN.)

RONALD REAGAN: Where's the rest of me?
(Dave starts to pace as well.)

DAVE: I started to make lists of what makes for a good monologue.
(MARSHALL stops pacing and looks at DAVE.)

DAVE: 1. Besides the ending, it had to be a story with act breaks and twists.
(1. LIKE A SCREENPLAY, DUH)

DAVE: 2. It had to have characters who changed.

(2. I WISH I COULD CHANGE)

DAVE: 3. It had to be emotionally true.

(3. WHAT THE FUCK DOES THAT MEAN?)

DAVE: 4. And yes, not always, but usually it had to be funny.

(4. I CAN'T REMEMBER THE LAST TIME I LAUGHED.)

DAVE: Meanwhile —

(SPALDING keeps pacing.)

DAVE: One of the other residency participants — a makeover TV producer from Philadelphia —

(RONALD REAGAN becomes the TV PRODUCER.)

DAVE: — and I decided to go for a bike ride —

(DAVE gets on a bicycle, as does the TV PRODUCER.)

TV PRODUCER: Spalding — Do you want to come along?

(SPALDING stops pacing.)

SPALDING: . . . OK.

(SPALDING gets on a bicycle.)

DAVE: So we went biking through the back roads of New Smyrna Beach, passing Confederate flags and chained-up vicious dogs. And then we passed some kind of smoke-belching factory.

SPALDING: Is that a recycling plant?

DAVE: Yes, I think so.

SPALDING: Oh God. That's what I was afraid of.

DAVE: He biked away as fast as he could.

(DAVE turns to the TV PRODUCER and they look at each other, but there's nothing to say.)

DAVE: Now back in *King's Row*, the surgeon's daughter keeps saying to Parris:

(The TV PRODUCER becomes the SURGEON'S DAUGHTER.)

SURGEON'S DAUGHTER: I have to tell Drake what my father did. He has to know that he didn't need to lose his legs.

DAVE: And Parris, who is now her psychiatrist, does everything in his power to keep this very disturbed girl away from Drake.

(The SURGEON'S DAUGHTER becomes PARRIS.)

PARRIS: It's bad enough that he has no legs. But if he finds out the surgery was unnecessary, it will be the end of him.

DAVE: And near the end of the residency, I talked to my spouse on the phone. *(into a phone)* I'm really stressed out about delivering my last monologue, Deb. Everything I've done so far in this residency has been shit.

(PARRIS becomes DEBRA.)

DEBRA *(into the phone)*: Whatever, it's just a monologue, Dave —

DAVE: Just a monologue? Just a monologue? YOU DON'T FUCKING UNDERSTAND; IT'S NOT JUST A MONOLOGUE, IT'S SPALDING GRAY AND NINE OTHER MID-CAREER WRITERS AND PERFORMERS AND I ONLY HAVE BITS AND PIECES AND NO FUCKING ENDING!

DEBRA: Who are you?

(DAVE hangs up, feeling very alone.)

DAVE *(to himself)*: Good question . . .

(He sees SPALDING looking at him.)

DAVE: When Spalding wasn't biking away from recycling plants, he did acting exercises with us to help us perform better in front of an audience, and I was even more lost; this was nothing like pitching screenplays.

SPALDING: Lay on the floor. Breathe deeply.

(DAVE lies against the wall, as SPALDING leans over him.)

DAVE: Being from the East Coast and from a repressed household, I had never breathed deeply in my life and I saw no reason to start now —

SPALDING: Breathe through all the pain, the anger, the sadness . . .

DAVE: What the hell was he talking about? Debra was right, why the fuck was I here anyway. I was wasting my time and hers —

(SPALDING lays his hand on DAVE's chest, with what seems like great pressure.)

SPALDING: Breathe . . .

(And DAVE breathes deeply and suddenly starts to cry . . . Almost weeping. SPALDING walks away.)

DAVE: I was humiliated, but realized no one had even noticed. And why had I cared anyway since all of us were already embarrassing ourselves baring our souls in our malformed autobiographical monologues? And why did I feel so funny. No, not funny. Something else. Something worse. I felt . . . Clearer.

(DAVE stands up.)

DAVE: Later, Spalding Gray finally told us why he was so anxious and distracted.

(SPALDING sits down at his desk.)

SPALDING: I was in a serious car accident. And then I sold my house, which reminds me of how my mother had sold her house and then killed herself. I've been trying to create a monologue about all of this, but I can't get far enough away from it to see that it can be funny, that it could have an ending. If I don't find the ending, I'm going to kill myself like my mother killed herself.

(DAVE looks at him disturbed. / DEBRA becomes the SURGEON'S DAUGHTER.)

DAVE: Now back in *King's Row*:

SURGEON'S DAUGHTER: If I don't tell Drake that his legs didn't need to be cut off, I'm going to go mad.

DAVE: And Parris, the psychiatrist who has built his entire life around helping people, is torn between the mental health of his best friend and the mental health of his patient. And this is the dark moment of the movie, because Parris is completely paralyzed.

(MARSHALL hunches over in his chair and wraps a blanket around himself.)

DAVE: Eventually, it became clear my father really was dying. His heart was in arrhythmia and his doctor told me —

(The SURGEON'S DAUGHTER becomes the DOCTOR.)

DOCTOR: There's nothing else we can do at this point. He doesn't have much longer. I'm sorry.

(DAVE takes this in . . .)

DAVE: So at the end of *King's Row*, Parris realizes Drake has to be told. And he says to Drake something like:

(The DOCTOR becomes PARRIS.)

PARRIS: I'm going to tell you something now and if you don't listen, if you turn your face to the wall, it will be the end of your life.

DAVE: And this is Ronald Reagan's crowning achievement as an actor.

(PARRIS becomes RONALD REAGAN.)

RONALD REAGAN: Give it to me. Anything you got to tell me. I can take.

(RONALD REAGAN becomes PARRIS.)

PARRIS: Drake, you didn't need to lose your legs. Your ex-girlfriend's father cut them off as an act of revenge.

(PARRIS becomes RONALD REAGAN.)

DAVE: And there's a moment where Drake just sits there. And then — *(RONALD REAGAN starts to LAUGH and LAUGH . . .)*

RONALD REAGAN: Did they think I lived in my legs? Did they think I am my legs?

DAVE: And he hugs his spouse and says something like —

RONALD REAGAN: We're going to start a new business.

DAVE: And it's implied they'll start making money and having sex and making babies and living a wonderful, happy life. Parris runs across a field to some girl he recently met and they hug. And everything's going to turn out OK for him as well.

(DAVE sits at his computer and types.)

DAVE: The night before the last day of the residency, I had been working on my final monologue — about the time I was four and me and Mary Ann Vreeland were in Mary Ann's bomb shelter trying to punch holes in her peach cans using my hilariously phallic toy screwdriver when there looming in the doorway was Mary Ann's father —

(DAVE stops typing.)

DAVE: And suddenly I knew I had been wasting my time.

(He moves away from the computer and picks up a pad of paper. He scribbles faster and faster. He crumples page after page. Until he has a single page of notes. He looks at what he's written and smiles.)

DAVE: And then it was morning . . .

(He gets up and appears to deliver a monologue. Laughing. Gesturing with his hands. Laughter from the unseen audience. Spalding watches. Marshall watches. The lights flash and then come back on.)

DAVE: I delivered a monologue about (you've probably already guessed) *King's Row* and my father. Afterwards —

(RONALD REAGAN becomes one HIPSTER, then another.)

HIPSTER RESIDENCY PARTICIPANT 1: I really liked it, Man, especially the unexpected connection between the movie and your father.

HIPSTER RESIDENCY PARTICIPANT 2: I hadn't even realized you had started the monologue, Dude.

HIPSTER RESIDENCY PARTICIPANT 4: It was like you were just talking to us.

HIPSTER RESIDENCY PARTICIPANT 3: Like we were having an intimate conversation.

HIPSTER RESIDENCY PARTICIPANT 5: I can't believe your father existed. Was he really like that?

DAVE: Yes, he really was like that.

HIPSTER RESIDENCY PARTICIPANT 5: Cool. I mean that sucks. I just have one criticism, not really a criticism, more like an observation: There wasn't much of an ending.

HIPSTER RESIDENCY PARTICIPANT 3: Yeah, he's kinda right. There wasn't much of an ending.

SPALDING: They're right. Your monologue didn't have much of an ending, but . . . It was very good.

(DAVE just takes this in.)

SPALDING: You could do what I do if you wanted to. You could deliver monologues for a living. David, you could be me.

(DAVE takes this in as well.)

HIPSTER RESIDENCY PARTICIPANT 1: Dude, you could be Spalding Gray.

HIPSTER RESIDENCY PARTICIPANT 6: Did you hear him? You could be Spalding Gray.

DAVE *(into a phone)*: I'm sorry for getting upset the other night, Deb. I delivered my monologue. It went well. In fact, do you know what Spalding said to me? He said I could be him.

(The HIPSTER becomes DEBRA.)

DEBRA: That's great, Dave, but do you want to be Spalding Gray?

(DAVE doesn't have an answer.)

DAVE: Well, I'll be home soon, and thanks for taking care of the kids, and you were right, it was nice to have some time to think about things in my life I hadn't thought about.

(DAVE hangs up.)

DAVE: Back home, I got busy once again with my parenting, my professor job, and my screenwriting and I forgot all about delivering monologues. Actually I thought about it all the time, but didn't do anything about it. I was reminded that I had also promised myself I would direct my own feature film. But it was never the right time, I didn't have the right story. I was about to start another writing gig. I was . . . afraid. / And a few years later, on the last day of his life, Spalding Gray went to a movie with his family, *Big Fish*, the story of a man trying to understand his dying father. After the movie, Spalding said to his young son:

SPALDING: I'll see you later.

DAVE: He stepped onto the Staten Island ferry. He watched the shore recede. He looked down toward the water. He bent his knees.

He hesitated a moment. And then he jumped . . . On the way down, maybe he was thinking:

SPALDING: Are there sharks in the bay?

DAVE: Maybe he was thinking of his son. Maybe the ending of his monologue finally came to him, moving, hilarious, perfect in every way except that it was three seconds too late to matter.

(SPALDING seems to reflect on that possibility. / Across the stage, MARSHALL is now very hunched over . . . Surrounded by various medicines.)

DAVE: Around the same time, my father was in a bad way. I flew to my boyhood home where he still lived to be with him. As usual, the blinds were shut and the windows were locked. But his legs were swollen from sores that would not heal because his heart was so weak.

(DAVE looks at him, looks at him, looks at him as MARSHALL breathes with labored Breath.)

DAVE: I love you, Dad.

MARSHALL: Remember me, David.

(MARSHALL reaches for DAVE with his hand . . . DAVE takes it. Weakly, MARSHALL makes eye contact.)

DAVE: I will, Dad . . . I will remember you.

(MARSHALL withdraws his hand . . . and looks away, exhausted. And then DAVE starts to walk away.)

DAVE: Although it had been 42 years in the making, his death seemed strangely sudden. I thought about *King's Row* and why my father had been so obsessed with this movie. / He had wanted to be Parris, who sacrifices his dreams of being an internationally respected psychiatrist in favor of healing his small-town friends, especially his best friend, his true love Drake. But perhaps unconsciously he knew who he really was: the surgeon, bitter he never achieved the respect he thought he deserved, and jealous of all those who might. And perhaps I was Drake, his unsuspecting victim. Yet *he* was also Drake, paralyzed by a fear he wished he could laugh at but instead overwhelmed him. / *King's Row* may not have been the greatest movie ever made, but my dad was right — it was pretty good. / I took a walk down the street where I had grown up, which I was always afraid to do since all our neighbors let their dogs run loose. / And on this day, indeed, a very large dog started barking at me from the front yard of one of the houses.

(An ENORMOUS dog comes towards DAVE. Threateningly. DAVE just stands there.)

MARSHALL: Remember me, David.

(The vicious DOG . . .)

SPALDING: You could be me, David.

(Barking FEROCIOUSLY!)

RONALD REAGAN: Where's the rest of me?

(Almost upon DAVE. GROWLING. GNASHING ITS TEETH! / DAVE holds out his hand, the DOG stops growling and barking, and sniffs DAVE's hand and then runs off stage. / DAVE relaxes. DAVE smiles. Lights fade on RONALD REAGAN.)

DAVE: I would make that movie. I would deliver that monologue. I would write a memoir and direct a play. I will do whatever the fuck I want to do. Because I am not my father.

(Lights fade down on MARSHALL.)

DAVE: And I am not . . . Spalding Gray.

(Lights fade down on SPALDING GRAY and then:)

DAVE: Where's the rest of me? Right here.

(Fade down on DAVE as he laughs.)

BLACKOUT/CURTAIN DOWN

Kids These Days

Like the Brady Bunch...
Only with drugs, alcohol, sex, and most of all
honesty

KIDS THESE DAYS by Rachel Robyn Wagner

Kids These Days

By Rachel Robyn Wagner

Rachel Robyn Wagner is a 17 year old senior at the Institute for Collaborative Education. She began acting education at the age of five, booked her first job at ten, and by age thirteen she was studying at the Lee Strasberg Theater and Film Institute. Her passion for writing began early in her high school career as a way to release the stresses of navigating through life while entering adulthood. When she found a way to combine her love of acting with her passion for writing, *Kids These Days* was born.

Kids These Days made its New York City debut on August 3rd at the St. Clements Theatre. *Kids These Days* made it to the final round in the Riant Theatere's Summer 2012 Strawberry One-Act Festival with the following cast, in order of appearance:

SAMANTHA	Sarah Sue Vallee
LEXY	Sydney Lynn Stachyra
JULIANA	Laura Pellegrini
MITCHELL	Jasai Chase Owens
GREG	Jake Robbins
CODY	Anthony Russo

The Play was directed by Rachel Wagner and Ashley St. Juliette.

CAST OF CHARACTERS

JULIANA, 17 years old, smart and secretive. She is beginning to let go of the childish perspective that everything is black and white and is beginning to see the grey areas of life. She is an aspiring writer and uses the experiences of her high school life to write her first book.

SAMANTHA, 17 years old, Samantha, tall and beautiful, is the seemingly typical prom queen and cheerleader. She has a lot more to her than she lets people know. She hides behind a façade to cover up personal trauma.

LEXY, 17 years old, she just moved to Boston to live with her dad who she hasn't spoken to in years. She is quiet and reserved. She tries to be positive but it is an uphill battle.

MITCHELL, 17 years old, a wall flower, he hides behinds books and computer games but secretly wants to be more like his friend Greg, the extrovert. He vowed that before graduation he would have his first girlfriend.

GREG 18 years old, Greg is the rebel of the group, the bad influence, the type of guy you wouldn't want dating your daughter. He jokes around a lot because if he's serious he would have to face his true issues.

CODY, 19 years old, a high school dropout, blonde, He is the typical prep school kid: he plays tennis, goes to parties, and breaks all the rules. He is Lexy's half-brother and the source of Samantha's trauma. He is the epitome of a womanizer and a narcissist. This is a small but demanding role.

Act 1 Scene 1

(Present day, New York, A messy typical teenage room, five friends, Juliana, Samantha, Lexy, Greg and Mitchell are all hanging out in Samantha's room they are frozen as Juliana walks Downstage. Juliana sits on the ledge of the stage with her feet dangling. She looks at the audience and takes a deep breath.)

JULIANA: *(JULIANA opens her journal and reads from it to the audience.)* It's about three months until I graduate high school with all of my friends and I feel exactly the same as I did a year ago. It's really weird how we spent our entire lives in school. We learned how to spell, how to read, how to do long division and multiplication. We learned how to dissect a sheep's brain, and how to write a 10 page paper at 1 in the morning. Our whole existence has revolved around our academic capabilities and how well we can prove ourselves in this stupid system. Everybody in the school makes it seem like graduation is this huge deal, like our lives are going to start the day we throw those hideous blue hats in the air. They treat us like our lives haven't already started, like all I've been dealing with is writing a paper on the fucking Cold War. For 7 hours each day we sit in that room as we have our teachers pretend like school is the most pressing thing in our lives. When they have absolutely no idea what our lives are like already. *(Juliana walks over to the bed and sits on the far corner of the bed, the spotlight fades and the stage lights come up. As she sits, the four friends un-freeze and they begin the scene as if they were in the middle of a story.)*

SAMANTHA: … So I just got up and walked out of class it was that simple. I clearly was not going to pass the test so why even bother sitting there for 40 minutes. Obviously Mr. Samson knew that I wasn't going to pass it. He handed me the test and was like "GOOD LUCK" in the most condescending way. God, he needs to get laid.

LEXY: I think you should have at least tried maybe he would hav--

SAMANTHA: Lex, if you have a B+ in math you get no say…

GREG: I mean Lex has a point Samantha, What happens when you're old and your looks fade you can't offer to sleep with—

SAMANTHA: *(Throws a pillow at Greg's head and laughs)*. Come on, we all know that was a stupid rumor!

GREG, LEXY, MITCHELL: *(In unison)* Uh…. Yeah. *(They all start to laugh, except for Juliana.)*

MITCHELL: *(Turns to Juliana)* Come on Jules, that was funny you can laugh too…

LEXY: Yeah really what is up with you? *(Hands Juliana a slice of pizza, she shakes her head no.)*

JULIANA: Uh, sorry guys I've just been so tired. I'm really tired so I should get going…

SAMANTHA: No! Juliana, seriously, this is one of the last few times we will ever have our sacred pizza parties, please just stay—

MITCHELL: You can't blame her, we had these parties when we were like 6. Where is the booze, the hot girls?

SAMANTHA: Not helping Mitchel…

JULIANA: *(Grabs her bag)* No I want to stay I just cant. I'll come to the next one. I have to make this deadline for the paper and I just really need to get home so I can finish Mr. Morrison's essay before I pass out.

MITCHELL: Shit… I didn't do that essay either

GREG: *(Talking with a mouthful of pizza.)* What essay…?

SAMANTHA: *(annoyed)* well looks like all three of you should go. *(Mitchell and Greg grab their bags and exit with Juliana, Greg returns to grab a slice of pizza then runs back out.)*

SAMANTHA: Looks like it's you and me Lex.

LEXY: *(sarcastic)* Shocker of the century. I feel like they always bail. *(Lexy picks up Juliana's journal that she left.)* Looks like Juliana left her journal here.

SAMANTHA: Ooh, Let's read it!

LEXY: Sam! No! We can't do that to her!

SAMANTHA: Come on, I know you want—*(Car horn is heard from O.S.)*

SAMANTHA: Is your stepmom here already to pick up the stuff for the auction…?

LEXY: Crap… Uh, look Sam, Please please don't kill me. But I kind of forgot to tell you that Cody was coming over to get the stuff for the auction, look I know it's awkward because you guys had a thing and all but he's my brother and you know he's going to be around a lot so I think tha—

SAMANTHA: *(starting to panic)* No, uh, yeah I understand. *(Starts to breathe a little heavier.)* The stuff is in the garage on the second shelf to the right, I would take it but I just don't want to break a nail, ha. So you should go, and help him and I will see you tomorrow.

LEXY: Wait, Sam no—

SAMANTHA: No, please its fine. *(Grabs Lexy's bag and hands it to her as Lexy walks her out of her room.)*

(The moment Sam's door shuts she falls to the floor D.S. and begins to hyperventilate as the lights fade. A flashback begins. The sound of house music and teenage laughter is heard playing through the speakers. The stage lights dim a little as Cody enters; a spotlight shines on him.)

CODY: Remember that dress you wore Sam?

(No reply from Samantha)

CODY: You looked really good that night, and by really good, I mean you looked like the biggest slut I've ever seen in my life. *(Samantha curls up into a ball on the floor and shuts her eyes.)* I mean the way you were dressed you were just teasing me. You can't have the reputation as the kind of girl who will do just about anything and then do nothing.

SAMANTHA: Stop…

CODY: There you go again, with this whole "stop" thing. Did you think we were gonna go upstairs talk about our feelings then braid each other's hair?

SAMANTHA: stop… *(Sam sits up, still facing D.S.)*

CODY: *(yelling)* NO YOU STOP. Stop denying it. You wanted it to happen. You were asking for it!

SAMANTHA: *(whispers)* You raped me.

CODY: Now, Sam—

SAMANTHA: *(Samantha stands up yelling, the spotlight on Cody fades. Cody exits.)* YOU RAPED ME! *(She turns around to see no one in the room but herself.)*

Act 1, Scene 2

(Enter Juliana she sits on her bed. Lexy runs into the room.)

LEXY: What the hell is this? *(Throws a journal at Juliana. Juliana picks up the book and stares blankly at Lexy.)* Huh? Do you have anything to say?

JULIANA: Where did you—Lexy did you steal my journal?

LEXY: Steal your journal? Who the fuck do you think I am the FBI? You have the journal on fucking lockdown, and now I know why! The only reason I have it is because you left it at Samantha's house.

JULIANA: You were never supposed to read that. What the hell is wrong with you Lexy? Have you finally lost your mind?

LEXY: Oh, so you didn't think I would find out about this fucking story your writing?

JULIANA: It's not just a story Lexy.

LEXY: Then what the hell is it? Why do I have to be a part of it? Why do you need to write all this shit about me Jules?

JULIANA: Look, I'm working on getting this thing published, this publisher Martha Warren really thinks that I have a good shot at—

LEXY: Published? Holy shit…. Did it occur to you to even tell me you wrote it in the first place?

JULIANA: I was going to tell you Lexy! Calm down—

LEXY: No. No! You have no right to tell me to calm down—

JULIANA: Oh my god! Do you realize the world doesn't always revolve around you? Don't you understand that I want to do something with my life—

LEXY: Oh and I don't? You don't think I want to be something too? I'm stuck. My entire life I've been stuck and no one seems to understand. You can't even write about me in your story without making me seem like I'm falling apart. I'm strong Juliana, I'm fucking strong okay? If I wasn't I would have killed myself a long time ago.

JULIANA: Lex, I really never intended to make you seem like that. Let me finish writing this. I swear, you'll love every single word of it. I just want to get people to think. I have all these ideas and I want people to hear them out!

LEXY: We all want to be heard Juliana.

JULIANA: Lex, I get it. You don't want me writing about you.

LEXY: No I don't think you do. It's not that you were writing me, it was the *way* you were writing me... It was disgusting! You think I can pretend like all this shit that happened never affected me? Because it did... I don't want people to read it and feel sorry for me. I'm not a charity case Juliana.

JULIANA: I never said you were! You really need to stop putting words in my mouth because it's not fair Lex. I need you to believe me when I say that in no way was I trying to hurt you. But your story is what's going to make this book great—

LEXY: Wow, Juliana... *(Slow clap)* props to you for making yourself sound like even more of a *jerk*. I don't know how many more times I can say this to you, but my life is not a story. My life is not fiction and it's sure as hell not supposed to be read for the enjoyment of others.

JULIANA: Lexy, I am not taking you out of this story. You can hate me all you want but you're in it, regardless.

LEXY: Who the fuck do you think you are Juliana—

JULIANA: I think I'm your friend, Lex! I love you to pieces but you need this story! If you can't see it now, then you'll see it later. But you need this story just as much as people need to read it.

LEXY: Who gives you the right to say that? The world is a really fucked up place that you know nothing about. But oh wait, I can't blame my parents for making me the way I am today because that makes me a victim! And if I blame myself, then I'm crazy. And if I blame no one, I'm lying! So what do you want me to do? Because if you have any chance of even putting my name in that book you better get it right.

JULIANA: Okay, so tell me how you want me to write you.

LEXY: I thought it was normal to have a mother that was a pathological liar and an absentee father who left my family and moved to a completely different coast. When I realized it wasn't, I don't know...

JULIANA: What? *(No response from Lexy)*

JULIANA: You can tell me.

LEXY: It sounds so dumb to say it out loud but it's like I constantly wondered why I had to be the one who had their entire life fall apart. I never really believed in God but I found myself thinking about if God really did exist and if he did, why did he hate me so much? *(Lexy starts to get worked up and emotional.)* I never thought that I could lose people in my life just by being myself. I was a person with a really fucked up life and a person who was going through a really hard time. People couldn't handle it. Why should they? I couldn't even handle it… I make people's lives harder just by being myself. Do you know how badly I wanted to die, Juliana? I wanted to end it all so badly.

JULIANA: I really had no idea what was going on with you. But I know you, Lex. I know you'll be okay—

LEXY: No, I won't be okay! I can't forget the day my mom barged out of her room yelling at me, blaming me for the reason she swallowed a bottle of pills. I was just a kid you know? I had to call 9-1-1 and when the woman on the other line said "9-1-1 what is your emergency?" I didn't know what to say. I was 12, and I was conflicted as to which emergency to elaborate on. I was tired, depressed, and on the verge of being mental!

JULIANA: I didn't know how bad things were with your mo—

LEXY: How could you? You think I just moved to NY so I could spend time with my dad? My mom would neglect me so I had to go. I was 13, and I cried myself to sleep every night. I had no childhood.

JULIANA: Shit Lex… I mean I can change the writing if you want--

LEXY: *(LEXY turns around to walk away, at the last minute she turns back.)* Yeah Jules, how about you give up the "I'm a perceptive writer act" and just be a friend for once. *(LEXY exits and slams the door. Juliana takes a long hard look at her journal and then tosses it off her bed. She falls back onto her bed feeling defeated.)*

ACT 1 SCENE 3*(Greg and Mitchell enter Greg's bedroom. Mitchell sits on the bed and tosses the ball back and forth with Greg who sits in a rolling chair.)*

GREG: I don't get it dude, Juliana is always so hot and cold. I know she wants me though. (Beat) You invited her and Samantha over right? *(Mitchell nods)*

MITCHELL: You think everyone wants you.

GREG: Cause everyone does… even you! I mean dude, I know you're gay you can admit it.

MITCHELL: Don't you think I would know before you if I was gay?

GREG: Nah, dude, sometimes people don't know till they're 60 years old and lying in bed with their wife that they had 10 kids with and then it just hits them you know? Like those people on that show… what is that called? Oh yeah, It's called "I Didn't Know I Was Pregnant". This woman was like, just straight chillin' on the toilet and out popped a baby! That could happen to you!

MITCHELL: I highly doubt I'll have a baby on the toilet…

GREG: *(Throws the ball a little harder at Mitchell.)* Very funny Mitch. Just don't be surprised when we're at our high school reunion and you're on the arm of some guy that looks like Tim Gunn or something, and I say "BRO, I TOLD YOU SO!"

MITCHELL: *(Catches the ball but fumbles with it. He holds on to it and doesn't toss it back.)* Wait whose Tim Gunn?

GREG: If you're gonna be gay then you need to know who Tim Gunn is.

MITCHELL: Dude, in all actuality I'm kind of into someone now… I really think I'm crushing o—

GREG: DANCING DONAVON AT THE FRO-YO COUNTER! I knew it. Dude, remember when he put that booty shaking video on Facebook, I knew you were staring at the video a little too hard when I showed it to you!

MITCHELL: Wait, what. No, I just didn't understand how a dudes pelvic—Wait okay, no that's not who I was talking about. I'm really starting to crush on Sam, as in Samantha, a girl…

GREG: Bro, couldn't you have picked someone a little more in your league?

MITCHELL: But I mean we're friends and all so I figured….

GREG: No, stop right there. You're friend zoned. There's no way out of it. I'm in the same boat! Juliana just stuck me in that friend zone. *(Smirks)* But in my case she's playing hard to get. In yours… well that's a different story. *(Greg stands up out of his chair and walks over to his desk and grabs a bottle of water. A thong is seen hanging out from Greg's back pocket on his pants.)*

MITCHELL: *(Goes over to Greg and grabs the thong from the pocket and holds it away from his body as if disgusted.)* Or maybe she doesn't like you cause you carry around thongs in your pocket, like a first class douchebag …

GREG: No, It's cool it shows I have some kind of wild side or something. I don't know this rocker guy on a TV show do it and all these girls were just swarming him you know.

MITCHELL: What…?

GREG: Never mind. Anyway—I think you need to reconsider your options here.

MITCHELL: Well can't you help me out? What can I say to get her to like me? Or what can I do? Flowers? Chocolate? No wait girls don't like calories... but if I don't get her chocolate does she think I'm insinuating that she's fat because she is so not—

GREG: Mitch, no, honestly. We would need the work of God to help you out here. Just give up.

MITCHELL: *(looking disheartened)* Uh, okay… yeah. You're right.

GREG: Shit, man, could you look any more like a Chihuahua being gang banged by a group of pitbulls? Don't look so sad, champ. You'll find someone… eventually… even if she's just on the internet… or is made of plastic and requires someone to blow her up… *(Greg tries to hold a straight face but ends up laughing.)*

MITCHELL: *(Angrily, Mitchell chucks the football at Greg.)* Shut the hell up!

GREG: Ow! Dude what is wrong with you?

MITCHELL: *(standing up)* Don't "dude me" I'm being serious!

GREG: *(standing up)* Oh my god, Of course you are because you don't know how to joke around!

MITCHELL: At least life isn't one giant joke to me! *(Imitating Greg)* Hi, I'm Greg and I try really hard to be badass by bagging any girl that I want, I also like to flunk school, and pretend that I don't know a THONG is hanging out of my back pocket! Life is one huge joke to me!

GREG: Yeah? *(Imitating Mitchell)* Oh, well my name is Mitchell and I'm the biggest failure on the planet because I'm an 17 year old virgin because my dad left me when I was a baby so no one ever taught me how to be a man!

(There is an awkward silence that falls over the two. Mitchell is visibly upset. Greg turns around as if ready to walk away. All of a sudden Mitchell charges and tackles Greg to the ground holding Greg's arms behind his back while he is face down on the floor.)

MITCHELL: Take it back!

GREG: Dude get off me, I knew you were gay…

MITCHELL: Is nothing off-limits? Do you think you can just throw all of these verbal punches at me and I'll just take them because I have no choice?

GREG: Mitch, dude, calm down, it was a joke.

MITCHELL: Because MY life is joke, right? The bastard baby jokes people make about me will eventually get old. But your life will forever remain a joke. You don't give a shit about anyone or anything. And when you go out to Sunset Boulevard and spend your last 10 dollars on a prostitute with chlamydia on a street corner I want you to think about this moment.

GREG: I would never pay 10 dollars for a prostitute! Of course she would have chlamydia if you paid 10 dollars, Mitch I'm starting to get a little worried about your life choices here.

MITCHELL: *(Frustrated. Gets up off of Greg.)* Oh my god, you don't get it… You do not get it! Life isn't a joke Greg. My life isn't a joke. Do I poke fun at the fact that your mother died a year ago? Do I find that funny Greg? DO YOU SEE ME LAUGHING AT YOU? NO! *(Mitchell turns around as if ready to leave. The same awkward silence fills the room before Greg tackles Mitchell to the ground in the same fashion that Mitchell did to him.)*

MITCHELL: What the hell! Get off of me!

GREG: Take that shit back!

MITCHELL: What?!

GREG: I don't think life is a joke. My mom dying is not a joke! Take it back!

MITCHELL: Okay, okay, I take it back!

GREG: Good!

MITCHELL: So, uh, who is the gay one now Greg? *(Mitchell begins to crack up.)*

(The both start laughing. Sam and Juliana walk into the room. They see Mitchell and Greg on top of each other on the floor. Mitchell and Greg struggle to get back on their feet, they try to casually make it look as if

nothing was going on. Greg scrambles to the bed and Mitchell scrambles to the chair. Sam and Juliana burst out into laughter, turn around, and exit the room.)

GREG: Looks like they *both* aren't going to go for us anytime soon.

MITCHELL: Yeah… Should we go after them or do you think we should just meet them at Sam's place later?

GREG: Yeah… Let's just process this and meet them at Sam's…

ACT 1 SCENE 5

(The entire group of friends. Mitchell, Greg, Juliana, Sam and Lexy are back in Sams room for their weekly pizza and hang out session. They all sit awkwardly eating pizza.)

SAMANTHA: So… Uh how was everyone's weekend?

JULIANA AND LEXY: Fine! (*They both stare at each other awkwardly then look away.)*

GREG: Uh yeah, it was good.

MITCHELL: Ditto. Uh, what about you?

SAMANTHA: Oh, uh yeah, you know… the usual.

(The group of friends freeze, Juliana approaches.)

JULIANA: *(Holds her journal in her hands. She looks at the audience.)* This is exactly what I was talking about. (*She takes a deep breath and pulls out her journal from her purse.)* This entire story is about the moments in life just like these stupid pizza parties. It's the moments where you are with the people you love the most in life yet somehow you still cannot fully be yourself with all your complications and all your problems… *(Juliana sits down.)*

This story is about the moments in life that define who you are. This story revolves around things that would be over-looked by almost anyone. It's those moments… those moments no matter how big or small that define who you are. *(Juliana walks over to her friends and looks at them in the face, she isn't just looking but she's seeing them. She's really seeing deep into who they are.)* You know, I look in people's eyes and sometimes if I look hard enough I can see their stories, I can see their struggles and their pain but as soon as they blink, as soon as they close their eyes it's all gone. Why are we so ashamed of our struggles? Why is it not okay to talk about them? They're trapped in the back of your head, they're trapped in your heart *(Takes one more look back at friends.)* and in your eyes. I know everyone has a story that they're dying to tell.

And my friends may not thank me now, but this story… it's going to mean something more than ink on paper. It's going to mean so much more than they will ever know.
(Lights fade to black.)

THE END

Justin Van Voorhis *as GREG* and Mallory Kinney *as ROSALINE*
in HOPELESS, IRRESISTIBLE by Keaton Weiss.

Hopeless, Irresistible

By Keaton Weiss

Keaton Weiss is an award winning playwright and director of both stage and screen. His other theatrical works include *The Meteor Season*, which premiered at the 2010 Strawberry One-Act Festival, and *Teddy and the Tin Foil Hat,* which received the award for Best Play at the 2012 Aery 20/20 Play Festival.

Hopeless, Irresistible made its premiere on September 14, 2012 at the Philipstown Depot Theatre in Garrison, NY. It was a finalist and Best Play nominee at the Summer 2013 Strawberry One-Act Festival at the Hudson Guild Theatre in New York City with the following cast, in order of appearance:

GREG   Justin Van Voorhis
ROSALINE   Mallory Kinney

The play was directed by Keaton Weiss.
Technical direction by David Markoff.

CAST OF CHARACTERS

GREG, a man in his late twenties.
ROSALINE, a woman in her mid-twenties

(An empty train platform. Nothing onstage except for a bench that could seat three, positioned just Right of Center Stage. No other scenery should be added, as the action of the play takes place in an ambiguous void. GREG sits in the middle of the bench, staring into space. He is wearing jeans, shoes, and a white button down shirt that is severely blood stained. He has a bloody hole in his forehead, directly above his nose. A moment passes, then, ROSALINE enters upstage right. She is pretty, but frail looking, with long hair. She's wearing only a hospital gown and a pair of hospital socks.

She looks around for a moment. She notices Greg, and stares at him for a long moment.)

ROSALINE: Excuse me, when does the next train come?

GREG: I don't know.

ROSALINE: *(looks around some more, crossing back and forth, up and down the stage)* Is there a schedule, or something I can —

GREG: No.

ROSALINE: There's no schedule?

GREG: No.

ROSALINE: But that's…Wait, where am I? Where are we?

GREG: I don't know.

ROSALINE: Well how… *(A moment of silence as Rosaline looks at Greg a bit more.)* You know you're bleeding? *(GREG looks at her sharply, as if to say, "no shit".)* It looks like you were…Were you…?

GREG: Was I what?

ROSALINE: Nothing. Never mind. *(She walks around some more, still looking for a schedule.)* Shot…Were you shot?

GREG: Yes I was.

ROSALINE: You were shot?

GREG: Yes.

ROSALINE: Well are you alright?

GREG: I'm fine.

ROSALINE: Well how'd you get shot?

GREG: I'd rather not talk about it.

ROSALINE: No?

GREG: No.

ROSALINE: Why not?

GREG: I said I'd rather not talk about it.

ROSALINE: Well who shot you?

GREG: I did.

ROSALINE: You shot yourself?

GREG: Yes.

ROSALINE: Why?

GREG: I'd rather not—

ROSALINE: Why would you shoot yourself?

GREG: Because I was feeling really hopeful. I was overwhelmed with ecstasy and anticipation for the bright future that lay ahead of me, and so in a moment of inspired joy, I shot myself in the head.

ROSALINE: Okay, look, I'm sorry. I'm just a little…But I'm sorry. *(A moment.)* So?

GREG: So what?

ROSALINE: Do you accept my apology?

GREG: I guess.

ROSALINE: So then why don't you say it's okay?

GREG: What?

ROSALINE: When someone apologizes, the polite thing to do is to say that it's okay.

GREG: Fine.

ROSALINE: Fine, what? Fine, it's okay?

GREG: It's fine. Whatever.

ROSALINE: I mean, I was just being concerned. I saw you had a large gaping hole in your head, and so I wanted to make sure you were okay. Obviously you'd "rather have not talked about it." But I pressed, and then you got really sarcastic and nasty, which was actually pretty rude, and so really, you should be apologizing to me. But I took the high road and said I was sorry, so I think the least you could've done would've been to tell me it was okay.

GREG: Look I don't want to get into a big thing here.

ROSALINE: Neither do I.

GREG: Okay.

ROSALINE: Okay, like "it's okay"?

GREG: It's whatever, yes. It's okay. Everything is okay.

(A long moment as they each wind down a bit. ROSALINE stops moving, stands just stage right of the bench.)

ROSALINE: So there's no schedule.

GREG: No.

ROSALINE: But how can there not be a schedule? You can't have a train station with no schedule.

GREG: You can, and you do, and we're there.

ROSALINE: Well how do you know when the trains come?

GREG: You don't.

ROSALINE: Well how long have you been waiting here?

GREG: Twenty years.

ROSALINE: Excuse me?

GREG: You asked how long I've been waiting.

ROSALINE: Yeah.

GREG: So I told you.

ROSALINE: Twenty years?

GREG: Yes.

ROSALINE: So when did you shoot yourself?

GREG: Twenty years ago.

ROSALINE: Twenty years— Wait, so…are you dead?

GREG: Yes, and most people figure that out a lot sooner.

ROSALINE: So if you're dead, then…am I dead?

GREG: Probably.

ROSALINE: So then where are we?

GREG: I don't know.

ROSALINE: Well it can't be heaven, unless you're like a saint or something.

GREG: No.

ROSALINE: Are you God?

GREG: No.

ROSALINE: Are you the devil?

GREG: No.

ROSALINE: So who are you?

GREG: I'm Greg.

ROSALINE: Greg…I'm Rosaline. *(She extends her hand for a shake. Greg shakes her hand.)*

GREG: That's a shit name.

ROSALINE: What?

GREG: It's a shit name.

ROSALINE: Well…my friends don't call me Rosaline, they call me Rose, or Rosie.

GREG: Still sucks.

ROSALINE: Rose? Like a Rose, the flower —

GREG: Yes I understand what a Rose is, I think it's an ugly name.

ROSALINE: Ugly?

GREG: Yeah.

ROSALINE: You think Rose is ugly? What kind of demented asshole thinks Rose is ugly?

GREG: The kind of demented asshole who shoots himself in the forehead. Perhaps you've already forgotten who you're taking to.

ROSALINE: Why'd you shoot yourself?

GREG: Listen, I don't want to talk to you.

ROSALINE: Why not?

GREG: Because I just don't.

ROSALINE: You got somewhere else to be?

GREG: Look, you think you're the first person to come through here and ask me all these questions? I'm sick of people like you. I'm sick of everybody.

ROSALINE: Well maybe you shouldn't be.

GREG: Shouldn't be what?

ROSALINE: Sick of people. Maybe that's why you're here, cuz you're sick of people.

GREG: What do you think you know about why I'm here?

ROSALINE: I don't know anything. But if you're sick of people, this is the perfect place to be, isn't it?

GREG: Alright, look, please, just leave me alone, okay? You're train will be here soon, and then you'll be gone. You won't have to worry about me, or why I'm here, or anything.

(A moment. ROSALINE starts walking around again, looking up and down the tracks on the right and left sides of the stage.)

ROSALINE: Which way do they come?

GREG: They come both ways.

ROSALINE: But how will I know which one's mine?

GREG: You'll know.

ROSALINE: How?

GREG: You just will.

ROSALINE: Will it say my name on it or something—

GREG: You'll know, okay? Everyone knows.

ROSALINE: But how?

GREG: Because when your train comes, you know it's yours, and you know you have to get on it. You ever feel that way? Like you know you have to do something even though you don't know why?

ROSALINE: Not really.

GREG: Trust me. When your train comes, you know it's yours, and you get on because you just have to. You don't know where it's coming from, you don't know where it's going, but you know it's your train.

ROSALINE: But that doesn't make any sense.

GREG: It doesn't have to make sense, because it's true.

ROSALINE: What?

GREG: Maybe to you it doesn't make any sense, but it does to somebody. And whoever that somebody is doesn't owe you an explanation.

ROSALINE: So I'm supposed to just wait here?

GREG: Yep.

ROSALINE: *(Looking downstage, into the fourth wall.)* Well, what if I go out there?

GREG: You can't go out there.

ROSALINE: Why not?

GREG: Cuz that's nowhere.

ROSALINE: Nowhere?

GREG: Yeah, that's nowhere. You can't go out there.

ROSALINE: Well it must be somewhere.

GREG: It's not.

ROSALINE: So what is it?

GREG: Nowhere.

ROSALINE: It can't be nowhere.

GREG: Why not?

ROSALINE: Because everywhere is somewhere.

GREG: Not there. That's nowhere.

ROSALINE: That can't be.

GREG: It is.

ROSALINE: But that's impossible.

GREG: You wanna try it? I'm not fuckin' stopping you. But it won't work.

ROSALINE: It has to.

GREG: No it doesn't.

ROSALINE: Well I'm trying it.

GREG: Go ahead.

ROSALINE: I'm going right now.

GREG: Good. *(ROSALINE walks downstage at a brisk pace. As she gets further downstage, she slows down, and just before the lip of the stage, she stops. She waves her hands slowly in front of her face, trying to feel out the space.)* What'd the matter?

ROSALINE: It's…I can't…

GREG: Uh huh…

ROSALINE: But it…

GREG: You understand now?

ROSALINE: No…I can't move.

GREG: I told you.

ROSALINE: I mean I *can* move, but…it's like I can't…

GREG: There are two ways out of here, and two ways only. There's this track, and there's this track. *(ROSALINE stands downstage, looking out into the audience for a long moment.)* You wanna come sit down? *(ROSALINE walks over to the bench. GREG is still seated in the middle of the bench. ROSALINE gestures to him, as if to say, "move over." GREG slides over. She sits. A moment passes.)* You know all the people who come through here, they all look…I don't know. None of them look like me.

ROSALINE: What do you mean?

GREG: I'm the only one who looks like, you know…Who looks like how he died. I men I still got this bullet hole in my head. No one else looks like that.

ROSALINE: Well not a lot of people shoot themselves.

GREG: Some people shoot themselves.

ROSALINE: Yeah, but not that often.

GREG: People shoot themselves. Or get shot. Or decapitated. Or eaten. I've never seen an eaten guy show up here like that. Like a guy who just got eaten by a shark doesn't show up with his arms and legs ripped to shreds and his spleen hanging out his stomach, you know?

ROSALINE: Have you ever met a shark attack victim?

GREG: No. That was just like, an example.

ROSALINE: Well maybe when you meet one, you'll be surprised.

GREG: No, I've met burn victims, murder victims…this one guy got stuck in a trash compactor…even he looked alright.

ROSALINE: Hm.

(A moment.)

GREG: So how'd you die?

ROSALINE: What?

GREG: How'd you die?

ROSALINE: Oh, I don't know if I wanna…

GREG: Come on.

ROSALINE: No…

GREG: Why not?

ROSALINE: It's stupid.

GREG: Stupid?

ROSALINE: Boring, I mean.

GREG: Boring?

ROSALINE: Well, yeah, I mean, you shot yourself in the head. That's way cooler than how I died.

GREG: Well how'd you die?

ROSALINE: Lymphoma.

GREG: Lymphoma…alright, well, that's cool. Lymphoma's cool. What's not cool about lymphoma?

ROSALINE: It's just not like…they don't even know what causes it. It just happens. And then pretty soon, you're dead. If I died from something like smoking, or drinking, or a drug overdose, or if I drove my car off a cliff, or if I got hit by a car that would be kind of cool. But this is just, I don't know. Bad luck.

GREG: Well getting hit by a car, that'd be bad luck.

ROSALINE: Yeah, I guess you're right. *(A moment. She looks intently at Greg.)* So when you shot yourself…like, what set you off?

GREG: Nothing. I didn't like anyone. No one liked me. I figured it'd just be a waste of time to stick around any longer. I mean what would be the point?

ROSALINE: The point is you're still around.

GREG: That's not good enough.

ROSALINE: Well who says there has to be a point? Why not just stick around, at least for curiosity's sake? See if they put a man on the moon, or cure diseases, or—

GREG: They already put a man on the moon, and they're not curing any more diseases, okay? The diseases are here to stay.

ROSALINE: You shouldn't say that.

GREG: What was the last disease they cured? *(A quick beat. Rosaline says nothing.)* Exactly. Polio. Polio was the last fucking disease they cured, and that's it for cured diseases.

ROSALINE: They've cured diseases since Polio.

GREG: Name one.

ROSALINE: *(thinks for a very short moment.)* Well, just cuz I can't think of one off the top of my head doesn't mean they haven't cured any.

GREG: Did they cure cancer? *(A beat. ROSALINE, disgusted, gets off the bench and starts walking away.)* Alright, I'm sorry, I shouldn't have said that.

ROSALINE: I don't know why you have to be so nasty.

GREG: I wasn't trying to be nasty, I forgot.

ROSALINE: How could you forget something like that?

GREG: I forgot that lymphoma was...you know...cancer.

ROSALINE: "Oma". "Oma" means cancer, asshole.

GREG: No it doesn't.

ROSALINE: Melanoma, Myeloma —

GREG: What about glaucoma?

(A quick beat.)

ROSALINE: Well what does it mean then?

GREG: I don't know, but it doesn't mean cancer.

ROSALINE: It means like a tumor, right? Even glaucoma is like a growth in your eye, or something, like a—

GREG: Look, maybe. I don't know what the fuck it is, but they ain't curing it. And I didn't mean anything personally, but people have these ideas, we're gonna cure disease, we're gonna feed the world, this and that. And they act like it's this big virtue to believe in these things even if they can't happen. Try to stop wars, try to stop crime, not gonna happen. There are people who try to and actually get paid to teach retards how to read! You can't teach a retard to read! And you can get as self-righteous about it as you want and wave your finger in the face of people like me, but it doesn't make you right. And it doesn't make you a good person. You're just stroking yourself and giving people false hope.

ROSALINE: What's wrong with having a little hope?

GREG: Nothing, if it makes sense. But it doesn't. I mean, the more you live, and I mean live, not watch TV or read, or go to school and hear a bunch of fucking no talent losers tell you how much potential you have and how you can do anything you set your mind to...I mean the more you see, the more you hear, the more you feel, the only reasonable outlook is total hopelessness.

(A moment.)

ROSALINE: You must write a hell of a suicide note.

GREG: I didn't write any fucking note.

ROSALINE: You didn't leave a note for your family?

GREG: Fuck no. Let them figure it out.

ROSALINE: Well have you seen any of them here?

GREG: No.

ROSALINE: Well have you seen anyone you knew since then?

GREG: No.

ROSALINE: What do you mean, no?

GREG: Would you like that translated? I mean "no, I haven't."

ROSALINE: But that's crazy! I mean, you've been here for what, twenty years?

GREG: About that, yeah.

ROSALINE: So no one you know has died in the last twenty years?

GREG: I didn't say that.

ROSALINE: But this is where you go, right? When you die?

GREG: I don't know.

ROSALINE: But the whole point of an afterlife is to see the people you love again, right?

GREG: There's no point to anything. Why do you keep saying that? It can be whatever it wants to be. I haven't seen anyone I knew from before. Not my mother, my father, nobody.

ROSALINE: Well am I gonna see my husband? Am I gonna see my husband again?!

GREG: *(mimicking, mocking) Am I gonna see my husband again?!* I. Don't. Know.

ROSALINE: Or my daughter? My daughter, I mean, Jesus Christ, where the fuck are we?

GREG: Why do you keep asking me the SAME FUCKING QUESTIONS OVER AND OVER—

ROSALINE: *(Losing it, tearing up.)* Because I'm having a bad day, okay?! I just fucking died! And you're not helping! I spent a lot of time in my life wondering what would happen after I die, as I'm sure everyone does, and I thought of a lot of things. But I did *not* think that I would be *chided* and *emotionally harassed* by some *deformed suicide case* on a train platform in the middle of fucking nowhere, so please, for both our sakes, just *lighten the fuck up!*

(A long moment, as Rosaline is emotionally exhausted and Greg takes her in.)

GREG: Alright, look. I'm sorry.

ROSALINE: For what?

GREG: For being, I guess, a little abrasive. But you know, when I first showed up here, I was alone. There was no one for me to talk to. No one for like a year. Then a few people started showing up, here and there, but when I first got here, I was by myself. I had to figure this shit out by myself. I didn't have anyone to talk to or commiserate with, to ask if there was a schedule, or where we were, or when the trains were coming, or anything. And to tell you the truth, I don't think I know more now than I did when I first got here. So really, again, I'm sorry I was rough on you, but please...I don't know anything...

ROSALINE: Well I'm sorry I called you deformed.

GREG: It's alright...There, you happy? I said it. It's alright.

ROSALINE: Like I'm one to talk, anyway. I looked more deformed than you when I died...I was blue, and shriveled up, and veiny... couldn't walk, couldn't eat... *(She runs her hands through her hair.)*...I was bald. I was bald. *(She starts crying some more.)*

GREG: What?

ROSALINE: My hair, it's...

GREG: Yeah?

ROSALINE: When I died, I didn't have a hair on my head...not even like shaved hair...things would've been better if I always looked like that.

GREG: That's an odd regret.

ROSALINE: It's true! You're such a steely-eyed realist and I'm telling you it's true. Because now, my husband, twenty-six years old, a widower...He has to raise our daughter with no mom...all because of me...because...because of this hair, this stupid fucking hair.

GREG: I don't understand.

ROSALINE: My husband told me this during our first dance. Not like, our first dance ever, but at our wedding, our first dance as husband and wife.

GREG: He waited that long to tell you?

ROSALINE: You don't even know what he told me yet.

GREG: Go ahead.

ROSALINE: And yes, he said he was saving this story for our wedding dance, because he doesn't really like to dance. And he's really shy, doesn't like being the center of attention. So he needed a really good story to tell me while we were dancing to take his mind off the fact that he was dancing in front of hundreds of people. Anyway, he said that on the night we met—we were at this club—and neither of us are really club people, but we were dragged there by different groups of friends...and he spotted me from across the room...I caught his eye. And he said he tried to look away as much as he could cuz he was too shy to approach me. But the whole night, he kept spotting me, out of the corner of his eye, I would always catch his attention, he said, because of my hair. He said the way the light hit it just a certain way, he just said I was…irresistible…and after a while, he just…I don't know, threw caution to the wind, I guess, and he walked over to me. That was just three years ago. And now…and now, I'm here talking to you. And if I weren't so "irresistible", things would've turned out better. He wouldn't be bereaved, and we would have this beautiful daughter who now has to live her life with no mom…everything would've just been cleaner, you know?

GREG: Well cleaner isn't always better…And you know, I don't think he sees it that way.

ROSALINE: Oh, please.

GREG: I don't.

ROSALINE: Don't try to do this now, okay? I've heard enough from you to know what you think.

GREG: You've heard enough from me to know I wouldn't make something up to spare your feelings. And I think if you asked him now…today even…if he regrets anything…I think he'd say no.

ROSALINE: How can you possibly think that?

GREG: I just do.

ROSALINE: Why?

GREG: It doesn't matter why.

ROSALINE: *(In a panic.)* Doesn't matter why? *(She starts breathing heavily, and darts downstage. She reaches the "nowhere" space and reached out, desperately, trying to escape, but she can't. Finally, she breaks down in tears.)*

GREG: Do you understand? *(ROSALINE calms down a bit, and looks back at Greg. A moment.)* It doesn't matter why. *(A long moment of still silence. ROSALINE walks back toward the bench and sits down. Another moment passes).* Hey, you know what I hoped happened when you died?

ROSALINE: What?

GREG: Now hear me out on this, and tell me if this wouldn't be the coolest thing. Okay, so you die, and like a big computer screen pops up, and it says you have like a million lives left.

ROSALINE: And what happens after the million?

GREG: I don't know, the Earth gets swallowed up by the sun or something. Or maybe there is no Earth and there is no sun, and you have an infinite number of lives, and for each life, you get to pick what you wanna be, and what time period you wanna live in. And you don't have to be human. You can be like a bird, or an ant, or even a tree, or a flower. Anything that lives, you can be. And so I chose to be white and middle class, in the 1960's…

ROSALINE: You went easy on yourself.

GREG: Obviously not *too* easy. But when I died, wouldn't it have been awesome if I got to pick my species, my gender, my region, my time period, everything? I'd like to live in the Old West, you know? Just once.

ROSALINE: I don't think you'd like that too much.

GREG: Well no, not for my only life. But that's just one lifetime. I'd like to spend one lifetime as a cowboy. Maybe one as a Chinese emperor, or a monk.

ROSALINE: I'd like to be a dog once.

GREG: Yea, dog is a good one.

ROSALINE: But not just any dog. Definitely not an abused dog. Like a really lucky dog who has really great owners, who would take really great care of me.

GREG: Or what about an alligator?

ROSALINE: An alligator?

GREG: Yeah.

ROSALINE: Why would you wanna be an alligator?

GREG: I don't know.

ROSALINE: That's a horrible life.

GREG: Yeah, but it's only one life, you understand? You have like a million lives.

ROSALINE: But that's a total waste of a life.

GREG: Wouldn't you wanna just one time be something that no one would ever fuck with? Top of the food chain?

ROSALINE: Be a lion, then.

GREG: No, lions…They got these flies in Africa, I forget what they're called, but they're extremely poisonous, or something. You get bit by one of those, this parasite gets into your bloodstream, and you're dead. It takes about five days, but there's nothing anyone can do for you. I couldn't live like that. I'd be looking over my shoulder all the time. Cuz a fly, you can't see coming, you know? Bears, mountain lions, shit like that you can watch out for. A fly, it comes and goes before you even knew it was there.

ROSALINE: So what? Because of some fly, you'd rather be an alligator than a lion?

GREG: Yeah. No one fucks with alligators.

ROSALINE: What about snakes?

GREG: What *about* snakes?

ROSALINE: They kill alligators.

GREG: What?

ROSALINE: Yeah, like pythons, or anacondas, or whatever…they wrap themselves around em and squeeze em to death.

GREG: Alligators?

ROSALINE: Yeah.

GREG: Maybe they do that to like, mice, or whatever, but not alligators.

ROSALINE: That's the stupidest thing I've ever heard. Do you know how many mice an anaconda would have to eat in just one day to stay alive?

GREG: Well whatever, they're not going after any alligators.

ROSALINE: Well how about this? How about you come back as an alligator, I'll come back as an anaconda, and we'll meet up, and we'll fight?

GREG: It's on.

ROSALINE: Good. I'll choke the shit out of you as an anaconda. *(They share a light laugh. A long moment.)*

GREG: Hey can I ask you something?

ROSALINE: Yeah.

GREG: If you knew something about yourself that no one else knew, and I mean no one—not you're mother, your husband, your kid, no one—and you knew that if they knew this one thing…that they would hate you forever. No matter how much they loved you before, this one thing that you know and that they don't, would put them over the edge…what would you do?

ROSALINE: I don't know.

GREG: Hm….

ROSALINE: Why?

GREG: I uh…nah…

ROSALINE: Come on, what is it?

GREG: *(Getting up off the bench)* No, it was stupid for me to ask.

ROSALINE: What, is that why you…

GREG: No.

ROSALINE: It is.
GREG: No it isn't.
ROSALINE: Yes it is!
GREG: No!
ROSALINE: Yes! It is!
GREG: Stop it!
ROSALINE: No, that's it. That's why—
GREG: Stop it!
ROSALINE: Tell me—
GREG: LEAVE ME ALONE!
ROSALINE: No, that's why you—
GREG: I SAID LEAVE ME THE FUCK ALONE! *(He darts quickly downstage, toward the "nowhere" space)*
ROSALINE: You know you can't go out there! *(GREG stops in his tracks. He looks out into "nowhere". A moment passes.)* You know you can't go out there...
(A long moment.)
GREG: I was driving in my car one time....and I was smoking a cigarette...and I never smoke, so I was...I was fumbling around with it. The lighter, and the pack, and the cigarette, the foil on the inside...I was fumbling around with it, cuz you know, I wasn't really a smoker... but I was just feeling so depressed and miserable, and so on my may to work, I stopped, and I picked up a pack of cigarettes...and I guess there was...I don't know, but I was...I was fumbling around with it...and...
(A moment.)
ROSALINE: What?
GREG: Well I...
(Another moment. Then, in the distance, the sound of a train whistle. GREG looks up. The whistle sounds again. GREG looks out toward the source of the sound.)
ROSALINE: What?
GREG: This is my train.
ROSALINE: What?
GREG: This is my train.
 (A moment, as the sound of the train grows louder.)
ROSALINE: Are you sure?
GREG: Yes. *(Another moment, as the train sounds grow even louder. GREG turns to ROSALINE.)* Look...I'm sorry.

ROSALINE: It's okay.

(As the train sounds reach their loudest point, the lights on GREG slowly fade to black. ROSALINE sits on the bench, alone, for a long moment, as the lights SLOWLY FADE to BLACKOUT.)

END OF PLAY

Home Care

By Phoebe Farber

Phoebe Farber is a playwright living in Montclair, New Jersey. She is a graduate of NYU School of Social Work with an MSW and Ph.D. She has a private psychotherapy practice and teaches at Montclair State University. Phoebe's plays have been produced at Manhattan Repertory Theatre and Apricot Skye Productions. She has had readings at Horse Trade Theater and Upper Mountain Ensemble. She is a member of The Dramatist's Guild.

Home Care made its New York City debut on August 17th, 2013, and was a finalist in The Riant Theatre's Summer 2013 Strawberry One-Act Festival at The Hudson Guild Theater. The cast, in order of appearance:

ANGELA	Vicki Kulkin
MRS. SCHROEDER	Kate Redway
DONNA	Sharon Dennis Wyeth
MS. D'NAPOLI	Rose DeBlasio

The play was directed by David Wohl.

CAST OF CHARACTERS

ANGELA, a homecare nurse, is in her fifties, no-nonsense, overworked.

MRS. SCHROEDER, a patient, is in her sixties. She is German.

DONNA, a secretary in the home care agency, is in her forties.

MS. D'NAPOLI, a patient, is in her sixties.

(*A therapist's office. ANGELA sits, facing the audience. She wears blue scrubs, and a hospital badge around her neck.*)

ANGELA: I have a lot of anger…I admit that…I think a lot of people do…they may not show it…but you can tell…if you really look…see my hands—like my father's—here—he had these—big, heavy hands, rough knuckles…same as me…*he* had a lot of anger—my father—out of nowhere—if he didn't like something—crack…I always wanted small hands—my sister has small hands…the fingers are a little chubby, but they have a nice shape…she took me once to one of those nail salons…I walked out…it's not for me…all that fussing over your nails…I couldn't do it. So, I have a lot of anger…what else do you want to know? What am I supposed to tell you…the report is right there…How long? I've been a homecare nurse for 17 years…12 at this lousy agency…I started out as a phlebotomist. What else? How long I've been so angry? That's a very personal question…a long time, ok?… a very long time. My free time? I have no free time…I see my patients, go home, feed the dog, do my paper work…that's about it……listen…let's get down to business, ok? Nothing personal against you…you seem very nice…very professional…but I'm a busy person…and I like being direct…so, tell me what questions you have, and I'll answer them…and we can both get on with our day…

(*MRS. SCHROEDER enters in wheelchair holding her finger in the air.*)

MRS. SCHROEDER: WHERE'D YOU GO?

ANGELA: Go ahead…I want you to put down how cooperative I'm being…

MRS. SCHROEDER: HEY!! WHERE ARE YOU?

(*Angela turns around and speaks to MRS. SCHROEDER.*)

ANGELA: I'll be right there.

MRS. SCHROEDER: You pricked my finger then you left me here--I'm bleeding…

ANGELA: I'm in the bathroom, MRS. SCHROEDER. I haven't disappeared—

MRS. SCHROEDER: I'M BLEEDING! (*Angela gets up and walks upstage to MRS. SCHROEDER. She takes her finger and measures her blood sugar.*) Where were you?

ANGELA: In the bathroom.

MRS. SCHROEDER: You wash your hands?

ANGELA: Don't be fresh…your sugar is high…

MRS. SCHROEDER: You were late today…

ANGELA: Did you meet with the nutritionist?

MRS. SCHROEDER: Who?

ANGELA: There's an order for a nutritionist to come see you about your diet.

MRS. SCHROEDER: Who?

ANGELA: Did she come?

MRS. SCHROEDER: Oh, that fat girl? No, but she kept yelling through the door…I didn't know who the hell she was.

ANGELA: You let her in, didn't you?

MRS. SHCROEDER: I don't need her—I have you!!

ANGELA: I'm recommending the pump for you—

MRS. SCHROEDER: How's Max?

ANGELA: He's a pain in my ass.

MRS. SCHROEDER: I don't want the pump—

ANGELA: It'll be much easier—

MRS. SCHROEDER: You hungry?

ANGELA: I'm always hungry.

MRS. SCHROEDER: Take some strudel—my daughter made it.

ANGELA: Tell your daughter—no more sweets! I'll see you Wednesday—

(Angela starts wheeling Mrs. M off-stage.)

MRS. SCHROEDER: What about tomorrow?

ANGELA: WEDNESDAY! *(She moves back into therapist's office.)* He didn't want to go for a walk today—Max--just lay there…wouldn't move…I've been noticing these small things…like, when I used to say walk—you ready for a walk, Max--he'd jump up and go straight for the door…now…he just looks at me. So, what, you never talk?

Oh, really? It's just me that talks? That's interesting…so, this is therapy…Italians don't go to therapy…we're very private…don't get me wrong…we're screwed up as anyone, but we keep it to ourselves…I talk to my dog…he listens, doesn't talk back…it's perfect…I find most people aggravating…you know what I mean? Most people are pretty stupid…Is that abnormal? To think that way? That was a question--what—you can't answer my question? I'm just trying to have a conversation—I thought that's what you do in therapy--Oh…let me get this straight…I'm supposed to come here and…tell you everything… you don't say a word…then you tell me when I'm better…and can go back to work…I get it…ok, that's quite a racket you got here. So let's get to the point…about the report…I didn't touch her…all I did was stand up…I swear…I didn't lay one finger on her…I have to go through it again? Please, just read it! I really can't go through it again…listen, I love my patients…don't get me wrong…I mean, they drive me crazy… but, I'm a good nurse---I ever show you a picture of my dog?

(She rummages in her pockets for a picture.)

That's funny—I always have a couple of pictures of Max with me…I must've run out…I'll bring one for next time…

(DONNA enters upstage, holding a chart. Angela's phone rings. She answers it.)

ANGELA: Yes? Who is this? I can't come now—I'm not working this week Mr. Franconi…another nurse is coming… I told you that-- you're WHAT? You can't go out—you're supposed to be home bound! That's why you have a homecare nurse—no, not the bank…listen…Mr. Franconi—didn't they explain this at discharge? If you're ambulatory— you don't need homecare—you can take yourself to the doctor.

(She moves upstage to a desk and chair.)

Listen, I'm not coming—I think Denise is coming to see you… but don't go anywhere… I'm telling her to check your shoes when she gets there…what did you say? You miss me? I'm your nurse Mr. Franconi, I'm not your wife. And you behave yourself with Denise—

(She hangs up. She sits, writing notes in a chart. Donna takes a step forward.)

ANGELA: Donna, I hear you back there…don't think I don't know you're there—…I hear you breathing…what is it, Donna? What little box did I miss?

DONNA: You didn't document the aide.

ANGELA: WHAT?

DONNA: DeMarco—you didn't write it in the chart…that you sent an aide in…

ANGELA: What does it say under "plan"?

DONNA: That you're sending an aide.

ANGELA: SO?

DONNA: But, it doesn't say it in the order…the box…42A isn't checked…aide…yes or no…you left it blank…

ANGELA: It says it right there! Under the plan!

DONNA: But the box—Medicare won't reimburse if the boxes aren't checked—

ANGELA: WHAT IS IT WITH YOU! EVERY FUCKING DAY WITH THE BOXES!!

DONNA: I'm just doing my job—the company has to get reimbursed—

ANGELA: REIMBURSED? I DON'T GIVE A SHIT ABOUT WHETHER THE COMPANY GETS REIMBURSED!!

DONNA: YOU'RE VERY SLOPPY WITH THE BOXES! WE WENT THROUGH THIS WITH MR. CORTEZ—YOU HAVE TO FILL IN ALL THE BOXES!

ANGELA: You got nothing better to do than worry that each of my boxes gets checked?

DONNA: I'm thinking of the well-being of the company!!

ANGELA: You really care about the well-being of the company? This piece of shit home care agency?

DONNA: How come you're so nasty?

ANGELA: Me?

DONNA: You're very nasty...

ANGELA: You want to know what's nasty? Six patients a day I gotta see—two hours of charting every night...you think maybe a thank you, a pat on the back? I get a note in my box every time I go under—checking on my productivity...and then I get people like you coming after me?

DONNA: I'll put it in your box.

ANGELA: Donna, do not put that chart in my box.

DONNA: You got to fill it in.

ANGELA: You put that in my box, I'm gonna light it on fire—I swear to God—then, I'm gonna watch the boss's face and say—you bitch—now you know what I feel.

DONNA: I'll just give it to you—

ANGELA: DON'T YOU DARE COME NEAR ME WITH THAT CHART—

(Angela slams the chart out of Donna's hands. Donna exits. Angela moves downstage to therapist's chair.)

You want to know the truth? Even though I didn't touch her—I could've... I could've killed her...It would've been easy—my thumb on her carotid artery...I had that much anger inside. Ok, so, what else am I supposed to talk about now? Anything? Really? You want to know what I'm making for dinner? Pasta Fagiole—you know pasta Fagiole? Oh...

you're not Italian, are you? I'll make it for you sometime--Max loves my pasta Fagiole—it's the best soup you ever tasted—I make it with the small white beans AND the large white beans…you won't believe it… What are *you* making for dinner? You probably don't cook—your wife cooks, right? You're smiling—I'm right…she probably does all the cooking, cleaning, you come to this nice office, wearing a nice suit, and just nod your head—that's a nice life…really…that sounds nice to me… having someone take care of you like that. Work? I've been suspended a week so far …It's strange…been working since I was 16--I grew up in Philly—my mother? My mother was not a warm person—she was sick a lot—her back, then she got cancer—always yelling—God, there was so much yelling in that house—so much anger…I think they must've hated each other—my parents—they were kids! He was 21, my mother was 18—they knew nothing! All they knew was their own miserable life growing up—and they kept doing the same thing…yeah—repetition… that's it…that's what they did—the same thing over and over--I guess you can't blame them—but when you have kids—shouldn't things be a little different? I mean, it's not just you anymore…half the time, I don't think they knew we were there…

(Ms. D'Napoli enters in wheelchair upstage.)

You know the funny thing? My mother? My sister was her favorite— but it was me who took care of her in the end. That's what I do—I take care of people—no matter what.

MS. D'NAPOLI: Is it open?

ANGELA: *(To Ms. D)* I told you already—

MS. D'NAPOLI: It feels like it's open—

ANGELA: I promise you it's not open.

MS. D'NAPOLI: It hurts—

ANGELA: *(Stands up, walks upstage, over to Mrs. D, takes out a tube from her pocket and shows it to her. Angela then inserts the tube into a port in Ms. D's back to drain the fluid from her lungs.)*

Look how I'm doing it—only half open--should I stop?

MS. D'NAPOLI: Go slow.

ANGELA: I'm going as slow as I can, Miss D. I keep my thumb on it, like this so it doesn't go too fast.

MS. D'NAPOLI: Am I done?

ANGELA: *(Angela checks the bag of fluid.)* I only got 100 cc's…

MS. D'NAPOLI: How much more?

ANGELA: *(Takes her stethoscope and listens to her lungs.)* We're about half-way—

MS. D'NAPOLI: You sure?

ANGELA: You tell me what you want—you're the boss…

MS. D'NAPOLI: My sister says I need to buck up—

ANGELA: Oh really?

MS. D'NAPOLI: Be tough—

ANGELA: Your sister has a lot of nerve.

MS. D'NAPOLI: You met her—

ANGELA: Your sister doesn't know what she's talking about.

MS. D'NAPOLI: She says she's never been sick 'cause she's such a positive thinker.

ANGELA: My father was like that—a real bully—then when he got sick at the end—what a baby!

MS. D'NAPOLI: You think this is my fault?

ANGELA: Your sister tell you that?

MS. D'NAPOLI: She says I need to think more positive—

ANGELA: There's more fluid in there—it would help you breathe if we got it out—

MS. D'NAPOLI: You think it's getting better? *(Angela takes her hand.)* Not even a little?

ANGELA: I ever showed you a picture of my dog?

MS. D'NAPOLI: You did.

ANGELA: I did?

MS. D'NAPOLI: Yeah. *(Angela takes out a picture and shows it to Ms. D.)*

ANGELA: Look at that face.

MS. D'NAPOLI: I don't want to go to hospice…You think I should go…to hospice?

ANGELA: You know what? Let's call it a day—we got 50 CCs— that's enough.

MS. D'NAPOLI: You sure? The doctor said to get all the fluid out…

ANGELA: It's enough for now.

MS. D'NAPOLI: You're leaving?

ANGELA: Onto the next Ms. D. I got three more people to see today.

MS. D'NAPOLI: I almost got married once.

ANGELA: Not me—

MS. D'NAPOLI: You're not lonely?

ANGELA: Nah—I got my dog—take it. *(She hands her a picture.)* He's a good partner--no questions, no stupid comments...all he wants is someone to love.

MS. D'NAPOLI: Stay for a minute—you want a cup a tea? I'll make you a cup a tea...

ANGELA: No time today, Mrs. D. I'll see you Wednesday.

(Angela wheels her off-stage, then moves downstage and sits in therapy chair.)

I yelled at the dog today—I felt bad—he keeps peeing on the rug—I think his bladder's giving out...I hate yelling at him...but the whole house smells like urine...NO PEEING ON THE RUG! I keep hitting the floor with the...you know...putting his nose into it and hitting the floor—NO PEEING ON THE RUG! He just looks at me like I'm crazy...he can't help it...that's what happens when you get old...the body breaks down...I brought a picture of him. *(She takes out a picture and shows it to therapist.)* He's cute, isn't he? He's really a mutt. You see the white along his ears? Look at that droopy face... ...no...you keep it...I have extras...You have a dog? You can't tell me if you have a dog? I don't know if you have a dog...you can't just tell me? Fantasies? I don't have any FANTASIES— here we go again. I just asked if you had a dog—a simple question—how many days I been coming here—you can't even tell me if you have a fucking dog? WHAT? It's more therapeutic if WHAT? I don't have any feelings about it...I just asked if you had a dog—I thought we were having a conversation...I talk, you nod...it's what people do...Oh--I forgot --you don't talk unless you get paid, is that it? How many fucking days I been coming here—because of that fucking report—how many more sessions until you decide ...what? I can control my anger? Well, good luck with that! *(Lights fade for a moment, then come back up to signify the passage of time.)* I was at the vet the other day...to see why Max is peeing in the house—maybe he has an infection. And there's a woman sitting next to me with a dog, and he has booties on his feet—he's a cute dog—so I ask her, "What's going on with your dog?" And she turns to me and says—are you ready for this-- she's putting him down—he can't walk anymore—so, she's putting him down. I couldn't speak. I'm around dying people all the time, but a dog, I take that harder. They're so innocent—they don't do anything but try and love you. So, I'm crying, she's crying, the ladies at the desk are crying. When Max and I got home, I made him get on the couch with me—the big lug—and I sat there—hugging him—that big head on my lap—"what a good boy...such a good boy." You look different today—you got a new tie or something? I don't know exactly—maybe the way you're sitting—I'm sorry—does that make you self-conscious? I'm sorry—I'll stop—I'm very observant—I can't help it. I wanted to say something—I know I can be rough sometimes—I'm sorry I yelled at you about...you know...the dog...I shouldn't of done that—if you don't want to tell me you got a dog, that's ok...personally, I think it's a little weird that you can't tell me such a little thing...but I shouldn't have gotten angry...I know you're trying to help—it's tricky...anger... isn't it? I've been thinking a lot—I have too much time on my hands I guess—I've been thinking about being a nurse—why did I choose that? What if someone came to me today and said—you have to choose another profession right now? What would I do? A long time ago, I thought I wanted to be a chef—you know I love food...I used to sit in the kitchen with my grandmother and watch her cook—I sat on this tall stool right in the middle of the room—probably got in her way— but I think she liked having me there--called me her helper. She'd hand me stuff—like a tomato and say, "Angie—tell me if it's ripe—smell it, feel it—talk to it". She had me talking to a lot of vegetables—but I was good—I was always right. She said every piece of fruit or vegetable has a way of telling you if it's ripe—the melon, it's near the top, tomatoes, it's around the sides...we made balls of fresh mozzarella—on Christmas Eve we made Bacala. My mother was a terrible cook—she had no interest—no patience--It's funny to think about, isn't it? What makes us choose things...and then our whole life...we keep doing it...even if it doesn't make sense anymore. Right, so, why a nurse? It was my sister's fault! She fell on her chin—went right into the edge of the coffee table when we were kids—I must've been 11—there was a lot of blood—she's screaming, my mother's screaming—for some reason, the blood doesn't bother me—I was completely calm. I got a towel, cleaned her up, got a bandage on it—one, two, three. After that, I was the one who took care of all the medical stuff. "Angela, get the bandaid, Angela, look at your father's arm, Angela, get me my pills." That stuff didn't bother me. You know the thing that got to me? Never a thank you. That's cruel...to never say thank you to a kid. When my mother got really sick—she had a colostomy after the cancer—you ever clean out a colostomy bag? I was a nurse by then, but still—that is not an easy job--maybe a thank you? A squeeze of the hand? Something to show me she was glad I was there—NOTHING! I didn't go to her funeral—I was too angry—a rough bunch of people, my parents—I hope he'll forgive me for it—I hope—YOU HAVE A NEW CHAIR! I knew there was something different! I like it—it looks very comfortable—it's good—you probably do a lot of sitting—you need a good chair for your back--*(Angela's phone rings. She lets it ring a couple of times, then answers it.)* Who is this? Yeah—you know I'm not working now—what, I forgot to check one of your boxes? Who? When? Where was she? No, I'm here…thank you for calling…I appreciate it. *(She puts away her phone.)* Ms. D'Napoli died…this morning. She was having trouble breathing; her sister brought her in—cardiac arrest…she was a nice lady… should have gone to hospice…THAT FUCKING SISTER…telling her to think positive…C'MON…I'd like to see *her* lungs filled with fluid, then tell me about thinking positive…she suffered too long…fluid in the lungs is very uncomfortable…you feel like you're drowning. I should've pushed…the draining I mean…I shoulda pushed for another 50— shoulda done it—I LEFT—why'd I do that? I remember the whole thing—she asked if she should go to hospice—I just got so tired--I couldn't talk anymore—I mean, of course she should go to hospice— but I couldn't get into it—I AM SO SICK AND TIRED OF TAKING CARE OF PEOPLE—WHAT ABOUT ME? WHO TAKES CARE OF ME?!!!! *(Lights fade for a moment, then come back up.)* I KNEW IT! I told myself—I bet he has a dog! I KNEW IT! So, what kind? Oh, they're very loyal…and smart…very smart…how old? That's good— you'll have him for a long time. What's his name? That's cute— Sigmund—you love your dog, don't you? I knew you did. I think dog owners are very compassionate people. You have to take care of them… they're like children. I'm glad you told me. Doesn't that feel good? To talk a little about yourself--now, we're really having a conversation— you're loosening up—you got a picture of him? What's this? *(She gestures in front of her, toward the paper the therapist is holding.)* AHA! I'M CURED! Back to work. So, that's it. No more anger. So, what happens now? I mean, with us? I keep coming? Oh…I don't come any more? Oh…next week is our last session…ok…So, that's it? That went fast—4 weeks—fast. *(Lights fade, then come back up.)* So, what do we talk about? Well, it's been an interesting process. I have to admit I was skeptical at first…but it's interesting to think about yourself…your life… my anger? It's still there…I have tools? What tools? Oh, the breathing…yes… count to five and take 3 deep cleansing breaths…that's my tool… Can I be honest? If that's the extent of what I've learned in therapy…to breathe…that's pretty limited, don't you think?…no offense…you've been very nice…but, really…that's what I come away with…count to five and breathe? I'm just saying…you might want to think about that…but you're the professional. *(She reaches in her bag and pulls out a Tupperware container of soup.)* I forgot—I brought you something—the least I can do on our last day—What? You can't take it? You don't accept gifts? C'MON—THIS ISN'T A GIFT—IT"S SOUP! I made you my pasta Fagiole. ARE YOU SERIOUSLY NOT GOING TO ACCEPT MY SOUP? I know…I'm breathing…see?… I'm calm…but come on! You gotta loosen up.…you told me about your dog…didn't that feel good? Try my soup…what's gonna happen…if you don't like it, you don't like it…I'll live…You'll try it. *(She puts the soup on floor in front of her.)* Here—I brought a spoon--it'll be the best soup you ever tasted. It's my grandmother's recipe. That tanginess—lemon juice…alright…how do we do this? Just say goodbye? *(She clasps her hands together and looks at them.)* Your hand is warm…good circulation… *(She unclasps her hands.)* It's been a pleasure.

(Lights fade slightly. Angela moves upstage to chair, sits, writes in a chart. Donna enters.)

ANGELA: I hear you.

DONNA: Question.

ANGELA: You miss me, Donna?

DONNA: On Romano—there's no discharge note—

ANGELA: Romano died.

DONNA: But you discharged him from services before that—*(Angela turns around and looks at Donna.)* You have to fill in the discharge section—the treatment, the plan…should I leave it here?

ANGELA: I ever show you a picture of my dog?

DONNA: Your what?

ANGELA: *(Takes out a picture of Max.)* Come here—I'll show you— See? That's my boyfriend…I'm kidding…it's my dog, Max…he's cute, isn't he? Here, take it—I have extras. *(Donna takes picture.)* You have a dog?

DONNA: Three.

ANGELA: WHAT?!! YOU GOT 3 DOGS? I didn't know that… how come you never told me that?

DONNA: It never came up.

ANGELA: What kind?

DONNA: Two beagles and a terrier…

ANGELA: Really…what are their names?

DONNA: Benny, Bula and Beatrice.

ANGELA: Wow…you ever take them to the dog park?

(Curtain.)

THE END

(Standing) MK Walsh *as INTERVIEWER,*
(Seated) Kelly Warne *as KRISTEN* and Adriana DeGirolami *as KATE*
in THE EXIT INTERVIEW by Betsy Kagen & MK Walsh.

The Exit Interview

By Betsy Kagen and MK Walsh

Betsy and MK met on their very first day of college at NYU. While at NYU, they collaborated on several plays including Tom Stoppard's *15 Minute Hamlet*. After graduating, Betsy and MK wrote and directed *The Murder Party*, which premiered at Manhattan Repertory Theatre's Fall Play Festival, in which MK also starred.

The Exit Interview made its debut at The Riant Theatre's 2012 Strawberry One-Act Festival on March 2, 2012 at The Hudson Guild Theatre, where it received the award for Best Play and where MK received the award for Best Actress for her role as The Interviewer. The cast in order of appearance was:

KATE	Adriana DeGirolami
INTERVIEWER	MK Walsh
KRISTEN	Kelly Warne

CAST OF CHARACTERS

KATE, A young woman who has recently died.
INTERVIEWER, A perky, annoying celestial being.
KRISTEN, A former friend of Kate's.

(LIGHTS UP. KATE enters looking disheveled, hair a mess, clothes wrinkled. She wanders around looking lost and confused. She checks to see that all her body parts are intact and in the process realizes that she has no pulse. Alarmed, she begins to slap herself in the face.)
    KATE: Oh my god. Why can't I feel that?
(KATE continues to slap herself in the face. The INTERVIEWER enters looking like a million bucks. Nothing is out of place, a great contrast to KATE. She carries a latte and an iPad. KATE notices the INTERVIEWER and jumps out of her skin.)

INTERVIEWER: Hi Kate. I am so sorry I'm late.

(KATE is taken aback.)

KATE: How did you know my name? Late for what?

INTERVIEWER: *(Laughs)* "How did you know my name?" Gets me every time.

KATE: Have we met before?

INTERVIEWER: *(Looking at Kate like she's an idiot.)* No. No we haven't.

KATE: What is this?

INTERVIEWER: It's just holy water. I'd offer you one, but you probably can't taste yet.

KATE: What? Why is that that happening?

(KATE absurdly tries to taste the air, making strange smacking noises.)

INTERVIEWER: That's attractive. *(Motions for KATE to sit.)* Please take a seat. Go ahead. Sit down. Right here.

(In a daze, KATE wanders to the sofa and slowly sits down.)

INTERVIEWER: Yayyy. Aren't these couches comfy? They keep saying they want to get new ones, but if it ain't broke...I mean, we've had them for an eternity. *(She laughs at her own joke.)* Eternity. So. How are you feeling?

KATE: Tired?

INTERVIEWER: *(alarmed)* Really?

KATE: What? Should I not feel tired?

INTERVIEWER: No. Feel tired. It's fine. It's not typical but it's fine.

KATE: Typical for what? Where am I?

INTERVIEWER: This is my favorite part. Katherine Elizabeth Price. You've died!

KATE: What?!

INTERVIEWER: I'm here to tell you that you're going straight to hell.

(As KATE erupts in tears, the INTERVIEWER hears something off stage. She addresses someone we cannot see or hear.)

INTERVIEWER: Oh, come on. She knows I'm kidding. *(To KATE)* You know I'm kidding, right?

KATE: *(weeping)* No!

INTERVIEWER: Come on. Live a little. That's just an expression. You are dead. I wasn't kidding about that part.

KATE: Oh my god. I can't believe this.

INTERVIEWER: I know. It's a lot to take in. Do you have any questions for me?

KATE: Will I ever see my family again?

(As KATE asks her questions the INTERVIEWER just stares back at her grinning.)

KATE: Am I going to heaven? How did I die? Who are you? What is this? Is there a God?

INTERVIEWER: All good questions. All valuable and important questions. Let's move on.

KATE: Are you going to answer any of my questions?

INTERVIEWER: No. Most people have questions and we find it's better to let them ask the questions. However, our policy is not to answer those questions.

KATE: Are you kidding me? Get me outta here!

INTERVIEWER: Okay, so you're gonna be one of the angry ones. Let me just write that down. *(INTERVIEWER struggles with the iPad.)* Sorry. This is the new iPad. Steve's released at least 8 models since he's been here. *(Hears something off stage.)* Oh, come on. She doesn't know who I'm talking about. It could be any Steve.

KATE: *(Shouting, getting up off the couch.)* WHO DO YOU KEEP TALKING TO? WHAT IS GOING ON? AND WHAT IS THIS PLACE?

INTERVIEWER: Not to split hairs, but I did already tell you that we don't answer questions.

(KATE throws a punch at the INTERVIEWER. Barely noticing KATE, the INTERVIEWER raises her hand and, without even touching KATE, causes her to fall to the floor.)

INTERVIEWER: Ah, Kate, Kate, Kate. That wasn't smart. Don't make this any harder than it needs to be. They saw that. And now I have to put it in your file. Please sit down. No more jokes. I want to get this over with as quickly and as painlessly as you do. I have a date later with one of the apostles. One of the really cute ones. And if you're nice to me, I'll put in a good word with one of his friends. I know you have a history of dating bad boys and Judas just broke up with Stephanie. Feel better?

(KATE crawls back to the couch and sits down.)

KATE: Judas. What a catch.

(KATE catches the INTERVIEWER'S disapproving eye.)

KATE: I'm sorry for punching you!

INTERVIEWER: You didn't punch me. You tried to punch me but I force fielded you. But I'm glad you're in the spirit of making amends. Because I have a list here.

KATE: What kind of list?

INTERVIEWER: I have in front of me a list of every bad thing you've ever done. FYI, it's taking up 18 gigs.

(KATE looks horrified.)

KATE: 18 gigs? How is that possible? People love me. I was head of social committee in high school!

INTERVIEWER: Oh my god! I am head of social committee in heaven!

KATE: *(sarcastic)* Oh my god!

INTERVIEWER: And if you ever plan on getting to heaven you have to complete your exit interview.

KATE: So, what? We have to talk about every bad deed I've ever done?

INTERVIEW: No. We find that this is a tough transition for people. Our studies show that divulging the entire list of one's bad deeds takes a toll on morale and, let's be honest, in your case would make the exit interview wayyy too long. So I'm going to select a couple of events here at random and we can discuss them and put them to rest. And then you'll have the opportunity to address someone you've wronged in person. *(perky)* And then that's it!

KATE: Who's coming to talk to me? That's alarming.

INTERVIEWER: Let's get started. *(She begins scrolling through the iPad.)* Let's see...where to begin on my very long list...watched Skinamax and called 1-900 numbers at sixth grade sleepover...

KATE: We were curious! Besides, I burst into tears right after I dialed. *(INTERVIEWER gives Kate a look.)*

INTERVIEWER: Stole Viagra from grandfather. Why?

KATE: I have no idea what you're talking about.

INTERVIEWER: *(suspicious)* Indeed. Put laxatives in Aunt Marge's coffee...

KATE: *(laughing)* Good times.

INTERVIEWER: Those good times can land you in hell, Kate.

KATE: Bad times! Bad times...is what those are...

INTERVIEWER: Oh here's a good one.

(The INTERVIEWER rises dramatically and looks out over the audience preparing to speak.)

INTERVIEWER: Event number one.

KATE: Oh god. What is it? Is it the time I gave my baby sister a Snickers Bar and she almost died?

INTERVIEWER: No. But that's on here.

KATE: I was only five.

INTERVIEWER: *(annoyed)* Look, Kate, we're not talking about that one. Right now we're talking about Maggie Walters.

KATE: Why?

INTERVIEWER: It was January of your 8th grade year. A cold winter's night. You were babysitting five-year-old Maggie. And you got a bit peckish. Despite the chill in the air you had a craving for Chunky. Monkey. Ice cream. The Walters happened to have a fresh pint in the freezer. You told yourself you'd only have one spoonful.

KATE: Have you ever tasted Chunky Monkey?? It's delicious.

INTERVIEWER: When Mr. and Mrs. Walters arrived home, the pint was empty, and they were not happy. It's Mr. Walters' favorite flavor after all.

KATE: It's everyone's favorite flavor!

INTERVIEWER: I don't care for the banana. *(Switches back to serious voice.)* When they asked you about it, you said 'I only gave Maggie two scoops after dinner like you said. She must have snuck down from bed and eaten the rest when I was doing my homework in the living room. Poor girl,' you added, 'she's going to have a stomach ache on the morrow.'

KATE: Whoa, whoa. There's no way I said 'on the morrow.'

INTERVIEWER: WHEN MORROW CAME, Little Maggie didn't have a stomach ache. What she did have was a strict new diet. Her parents thought she was a compulsive eater. She hasn't had ice cream, candy, or any fun since. She's eighteen now. AND LITTLE MAGGIE'S STILL HUNGRY. *(To offstage.)* What? I'm not being dramatic! She could be hungry....today....we don't know.

KATE: Oh god. I had no idea it affected her that way.

INTERVIEWER: Gimme a break. You felt so guilty for what you did, you never babysat for them again.

KATE: You're right. I feel bad! Is Maggie the one I have to face?

INTERVIEWER: Oh god, no. This is nothing compared...we'll get to that later. One down. Two to go!

KATE: This is awful.

INTERVIEWER: I know. It's a real character builder though. And the good news is we're a third of the way through.

(The INTERVIEWER scrolls through the iPad with her eyes closed again.)

INTERVIEWER: Ooh. Here's a doozy. April. Of your sophomore year of college. You killed a man.

KATE: WHAT?? I NEVER KILLED ANYONE! WHAT? CHECK THAT AGAIN.

(The INTERVIEWER refers to her iPad.)

INTERVIEWER: *(reading)* She. Killed. A. Man.

KATE: *(beginning to cry, talking to herself)* Oh my god. I never killed anyone...did I? I would've remembered. I didn't know.

(As KATE really begins to lose it, the INTERVIEWER cracks up.)

INTERVIEWER: I'm kidding!

KATE: WHAT!?

INTERVIEWER: Yeah! I'm just jokin'! You should have seen yourself. *(Mocking KATE.)* What? I never killed anybody. Wait, did I? Wah blah blah blah!

KATE: Oh my god. I'm like sweating here.

INTERVIEWER: Most people find that funny. Comic relief? Whatever. Tough crowd. Moving on. *(She scrolls through her iPad.)* Let's see here...The time the dog ate your bag of marijuana...and died...

KATE: There was never any proof that was how he died! He was old.

INTERVIEWER: No, honey. It was the weed. *(She keeps scrolling.)* Hit a parked car...drove away...

KATE: I never...

INTERVIEWER: Don't bother... *(Keeps scrolling.)* Oh, here's a good one of my favorites.

(The INTERVIEWER rises again and becomes extremely dramatic, booming voice and all.)

INTERVIEWER: February of your senior year of high school--

KATE: What is that accent? Is it supposed to be British or.....

(The INTERVIEWER tries to crush her exasperation.)

INTERVIEWER: It's my district attorney voice. *(Back to the voice.)* It was February of your senior year of high school. You had old Mr. Shapiro for history. Mr. Shapiro was known for his long boring lectures and senile tendencies. One day you decided, TO HELL WITH THE OLD MAN AND THE FRENCH REVOLUTION. You weren't going to class. Apparently Mr. Shaprio wasn't as senile as you thought because he noticed your absence and reported it to the dean. Do you remember what happened next, Kate?

KATE: *(ashamed)* The dean came to talk to me about cutting class.

INTERVIEWER: And what did you tell her, Kate?

KATE: That I was in class.

INTERVIEWER: *(incredulous)* AND SHE BELIEVED YOU?!

KATE: Yeah.

INTERVIEWER: But WHY? Why did she believe such an outrageous story?

KATE: Because I had never skipped class before.

INTERVIEWER: AND!?

KATE: And I told her Mr. Shapiro must have been confused.

INTERVIEWER: EXACTLY! Surely the ladies and gentlemen of the jury can see—

KATE: What jury? I don't see a jury.

(The INTERVIEWER tries to collect herself but is clearly furious with KATE.)

INTERVIEWER: *(to herself)* See God in everyone. See God in everyone. *(to KATE)* Surely the jury--which exists and is present--can see that you used your reputation as a reliable student and your poor teacher's senility to escape punishment. Your dean didn't question your integrity for a second, DID SHE!?

KATE: No.

INTERVIEWER: And I bet you didn't know that that was Mr. Shapiro's last year at the school, did you?

KATE: They fired him??

INTERVIEWER: *(Screaming in KATE'S bewildered face.)* NO!!! HE RETIRED TO BOCA. HE WAS WAY TOO OLD TO BE TEACHING!!!! WHICH IS IRRELEVANT!!!! The point is you shouldn't have done that.

KATE: You're right. *(Beat)* So I'm not going to face Mr. Shapiro either, right?

INTERVIEWER: No, what? I told you. He retired to Boca. He has a bridge game at 3:00pm with Mr. Mandelbaum. They're in the semi-finals.

KATE: Okay. So...what's the last one? Who am I meeting?

INTERVIEWER: I think if you really thought about it you would know.

KATE: I already guessed the Snickers thing! She almost died! She's allergic to peanuts now!

INTERVIEWER: Molly isn't angry about the stupid Snickers Bar! She was only 8 months old. Molly worships you for some reason unbeknownst to me. You don't have any amends to make to her.

KATE: Okay. Who then?

INTERVIEWER: KRISTEN GRAHAM COME ON DOWN!!!

(KATE is horror-struck. KRISTEN enters looking just as confused as KATE did.)

KRISTEN: What is this place?

(KRISTEN blinks a few times and finally sees KATE. She is unpleased.)

INTERVIEWER: Surprise! It's your former best friend Kristeeeeennnnn!!!

KATE: Best friends? That's a little generous.

KRISTEN: Oh please, Kate. We've known each other since the summer we gave Molly that Snickers Bar.

KATE: Yeah, thanks for almost killing my sister, Kristen.

KRISTEN: Please, it was your idea. You were all, 'Let's see what happens! She only has one tooth!'

KATE: I was only five!

INTERVIEWER: Aw, friends since you were five. Kate and Kristen. Kristen and Kate. The two K's. Oh my god! I bet everyone called you K-squared!

KRISTEN: *(feigning enthusiasm)* Oh my god!... No one called us that.

(The INTERVIEWER is offended and already doesn't like Kristen at all.)

KATE: Ignore her. She's very annoying.

KRISTEN: Who the hell is she?

KATE: I don't really know. I've been talking to her for... *(To the INTERVIEWER)* How long have I been here?

INTERVIEWER: I'm just gonna step aside and just let you two hash it out.

(The INTERVIEWER walks to the side and starts playing a game on her ipad. KATE and KRISTEN stand in silence for a moment. It's awkward.)

KATE: This is clearly very awkward.

INTERVIEWER: Yeah it is.

KATE: I thought you weren't participating.

INTERVIEWER: Pretend like I'm not here.

KRISTEN: So...speaking of awkward...are you dead?

KATE: Um. Yeah.

(KRISTEN laughs, delighted that KATE is dead. Then a realization hits her.)

KRISTEN: Oh my god! Am I dead?

KATE: Uh, I don't know. Let me check. *(To INTERVIEWER)* Is she dead?

INTERVIEWER: First you tell me to shut up. Now you're asking me questions, which you know it's not my policy to answer—

KRISTEN/KATE: *(simultaneously)* JUST TELL ME IF I'M DEAD!/ Just tell her if she's dead.

INTERVIEWER: Feisty! No, you're not dead...yet. You won't remember any of this happening. This is Kate's exit interview. Your exit interview isn't for decades. And I hope to god I'm not your interviewer because your attitude is worse than hers. Now get talking. Kate, remember I have a date. *(Whispering to KRISTEN.)* With an apostle. *(The INTERVIEWER goes back to reading her iPad.)*

KATE: I'm sorry about this. I don't even know why you're here.

KRISTEN: I can think of a few reasons.

KATE: What is that supposed to mean?

KRISTEN: I don't know. It looks like this is your opportunity to right wrongs, tie up loose ends. Obviously the universe thinks you need to make amends with me to move on.

KATE: Wow! How many exit interviews have you been to?

KRISTEN: This is my first one but it's a pretty simple idea.

INTERVIEWER: If I may. Technically, Kristen, you may have been to others. They're designed so that you won't remember them.

KATE: So then—

INTERVIEWER: *(doing a "talk to the hand")* No. Pretend like I'm not even here.

KATE: *(Looking at KRISTEN.)* Fine. Sorry for everything I ever did to you...Ever.

(Beat)

KRISTEN: Whatever.

KATE: *(to INTERVIEWER)* Are we good?

INTERVIEWER: Yeah, you can go. Bye Kristen!

KRISTEN: Great. Seeya.

(KRISTEN exits.)

KATE: Oh my god. Is she not the worst? I mean, the worst. She used to pull this shit all the time when we were friends. On earth. As it is in heaven. Suffice it to say, when she has her...one of these things, I will be here.

(KRISTEN enters.)

KRISTEN: What the F? I'm still here.

KATE: What! She's still here!

INTERVIEWER: Ah, K-squared. You two are funny. Did you really think it would be that easy? Now, I want you to sit down and dig up more drama than I saw between Voldemort and Harry Potter.

(A beat as this information settles.)

INTERVIEWER: Yeah. It's real.

(KATE and KRISTEN sit down.)

KATE: All right. I guess we really have to do this. So...why do you think you're here?

KRISTEN: I know why I'm here, Kate. I'm here because when you were alive--which you no longer are--you were a heinous bitch to me. Could that be it?

KATE: What? We grew apart. It happens. Get over it.

KRISTEN: We didn't just grow apart.

KATE: We went to different colleges. It's not like I just woke up one morning and decided to stop being friends with you.

KRISTEN: Really? Because it seems like that's exactly what it felt like.

KATE: A lot of people lose touch with their friends when they go to college. It's natural. I wasn't being malicious.

KRISTEN: We'd been friends since we were five. And yes, growing apart happens. What you did to me was a lot more than the typical friends growing apart.

KATE: What did I do to you?

(KRISTEN rises.)

KRISTEN: You didn't do anything to me. Or for me, and that is the point. When my dad died you didn't come to the funeral, you didn't call me, you didn't text me. Nothing. In fact, this is the first interaction I've had with you since it happened. You had to die before we could address this.

KATE: We had stopped being friends way before that happened.

KRISTEN: What? Six months? I don't care if it's five years. When a parent dies, you show up. At the very least, you pick up the goddamn phone. You know what? It's too late to apologize.

(In this very emotional moment, the INTERVIEWER begins to sing "Apologize" by One Republic. KATE and KRISTEN stare at her aghast.)

KRISTEN/KATE: *(simultaneously)* SHUT UP!

INTERVIEWER: Um...Okay.

KRISTEN: Look, I don't give a shit if you feel sorry about this. I'm over it. I'm just betting that you're not. And that's why I'm here.

KATE: *(to INTERVIEWER)* Is that why she's here?

INTERVIEWER: She isn't here for idle chitchat, Kate. Do you have any idea the paperwork involved in getting a living human being here? Frankly, you're wasting both of our time. *(To offstage.)* Yeah, I know. Believe me. I know. She's not getting it. *(To KATE)* Okay, I'm getting word from above that you're not ready to move on. This is over. We'll have to reschedule. I have availability in...*(Scrolls through iPad)*...three millenia. Just wait here. So nice meeting you both. Not really.

KATE: Whoa, whoa. Wait! Wait. Get back here. Let's like...do this.

(The INTERVIEWER stands tentatively near the exit.)

KATE: Kristen, please sit down. It was six months. Almost to the day. And I remember the day. When we first got to school, I was so busy with my new stupid college kid life. You would call me, and I would let a day go by without calling you back. And then a week would go by. And then a month. And then it was six months, and your dad was dead. I couldn't face you.

KRISTEN: That's a bullshit excuse.

KATE: I'm not saying it isn't. I'm just telling you what happened. Obviously, as evidenced by you being here I've felt horrible about this since. I guess it's my biggest regret. *(To INTERVIEWER)* Right?

INTERVIEWER: So many to choose from with you.

KATE: *(To KRISTEN, indicating the INTERVIEWER.)* I mean, this. I'm dealing with it every second.

INTERVIEWER: I'm kidding! Yes, of course this is your biggest regret. You're a really shitty friend.

KRISTEN: Well, she wasn't. Until then.

KATE: Look, that was a really awful thing I did to you. And I'm really, really sorry.

KRISTEN: Well, you spent the rest of your life suffering the guilt of it. That's pretty satisfying.

KATE: *(chuckles)* I'm glad my misery brings you happiness.

KRISTEN: A little bit...not a lot...but...it's there.

KATE: *(laughing)* Can we just start over?

(KRISTEN looks at KATE for a moment.)

KRISTEN: Um. Actually I don't know. *(To the INTERVIEWER.)* Can we?

INTERVIEWER: What is wrong with you? No. You're alive. And you're dead and it just doesn't...no.

KATE: Oh yeah. Well, will I see her again when she dies?

KRISTEN: Which won't be any time soon.

INTERVIEWER: Sure...actually I don't know. That's not my call. I have no idea if you'll ever see each other again. Kristen, you have to go.

KRISTEN: Okay.

(KRISTEN and KATE both get up. They hug. The INTERVIEWER is moved and joins the hug.)

INTERVIEWER: Girls, all three of us. I think we need it.

(The hug is now extremely awkward. When they break away KATE and KRISTEN take a moment to recover.)

KATE: Well, have a nice life.

KRISTEN: Yeah, you too...no...you can't...because....Have fun. Being dead. Okay, I have to go.

(KRISTEN begins to leave.)

KRISTEN: I don't know how to go.

INTERVIEWER: Right through there.

KRISTEN: Oh, say hi to my dad.

INTERVIEWER: If you can get to him. That guy's popular up here.

(More confused than ever, KRISTEN exits.)

KATE: So how'd I do?

INTERVIEWER: Well, despite rocky, obnoxious beginnings, you turned out to be pretty good at this.

KATE: So what happens now?

INTERVIEWER: In the spirit of never answering questions, I'm just going to say that you'll have to find out what's next for yourself. Not to worry though, wardrobe will be here to collect you. You don't have to spend the rest of eternity in that outfit.

KATE: I kinda like this outfit.

INTERVIEWER: Me too. Love it. Where'd you get it? I have to go. *(The INTERVIEWER begins to leave.)*

INTERVIEWER: Oh, and Kate?

KATE: Yeah?

INTERVIEWER: Just so you know, for every gig of bad stuff, there was at least ten gigs of good. The bad stuff's just more entertaining for me. You understand.

(KATE nods. The INTERVIEWER exits. KATE takes a deep breath and sits down. She looks around and waits peacefully to see what's next. LIGHTS OUT.)

THE END

PAULA'S VISITOR by Keith Miles Filangieri.

Paula's Visitor
By Keith Miles Filangieri

Keith Miles Filangieri is a current playwriting student from the Acting Studio, Inc, New York and a member of the Dramatists Guild of America, Inc. Keith graduated from Stony Brook University with a Bachelor of Arts in Theatre and was a literary associate at the Abingdon Theatre. Aside from writing for the stage, Keith currently works for South Oaks Hospital, Amityville, New York, as a job coach, training autistic high school students for employment.

Paula's Visitor started off as a 10-minute play, submitted to the Stony Brook Playwriting Competition in the spring of 2010. It was later extended to a One-Act and was read at the Acting Studio in the spring of 2012. During that summer, *Paula's Visitor* had been performed at The Riant Theatre's Strawberry One-Act Festival with the following cast, in order of appearance:

JIM	Bjorn Strigel
DR. SOW	Jarvis Smith
DAVID	Michael Orlandi
LANA	Courtney Cook
FREDDY	Steve Anderson
PAULA	Michelle Lupo
VISITOR	Orlando Rivera

The play was directed by Lawrence Schwartz.

CAST OF CHARACTERS

JIM, Paula's husband and businessman; is in his early 30s; Caucasian.
DR. SOW, a medical doctor and biologist on the tour; is in his mid-40s; of African descent.
DAVID, the tour guide; is in his mid-30s; Caucasian.

LANA, a newly-wed and tourist; is in her mid-20s.

FREDDY, Lana's newly-wed husband; is in his mid-20s.

PAULA, an American tourist and actress gone blind; is in her late 20s; Caucasian.

VISITOR, a stranger who is supposedly one of the tourists; is in his mid-20s; referred as Travis.

SCENE 1

(A jungle in South Africa. Daylight, late morning. A campsite with tents in a clearing. One is far upstage center. On center stage is a pile of wood where a fire can be made. Around it are plastic chairs. JIM enters from far upstage right. He is a Caucasian man in his early 30s. He appears to be concerned about something. As he sits down by the pile of wood, DR. SOW exits from the tent upstage and approaches him. He is an African man in his mid-40s, carrying a first aid kit.)

DR. SOW: Jim? *(JIM immediately gets up.)*

JIM: Well…how is she?

DR. SOW: She's doing much better. The eye drops seem to be working. But…she's still blind.

JIM: This is only temporary, right?

DR. SOW: Yes. The *Euphorbia cooperi* is a very –

JIM: I'm sorry, the what?

DR. SOW: The *Euphorbia cooperi.* It's the name of the plant that irritated her eyes. It's quite a vicious one. It releases white latex that can produce blisters on the skin of whom ever encounters it. It can also cause infection to the eyes and throat. Mrs. Powers unfortunately went through all of those symptoms.

JIM: So, now what?

DR. SOW: Now, all she has to do is recover. The worst is over. She's no longer in pain. Once her sight is back, she'll be fully cured.

JIM: And when will that be?

DR. SOW: It's…hard to tell at the moment. It could be in minutes, hours, a day or two. At most, three days. She demands that she wears the blindfold. She doesn't want anyone to see the blisters around her eyes.

JIM: *(Sighs.)* Boy, what a trip this turned out to be. Promised her we'd have a good time. I can only imagine how miserable she must be, right now.

DR. SOW: I strongly recommend her not to go on the safari. It's better if she stays here for the day.

JIM: I guess you're right. Oh, God, this marriage is not gonna last.

DR. SOW: If you don't mind me asking, how long have you two been married?

JIM: Four years. But ever since my promotion as a bank manager and Paula's acting career, we haven't had much time together.

DR. SOW: *(Enthusiastically.)* She's an actress?

JIM: Yeah, she's worked on stage for quite awhile, now.

DR. SOW: Broadway?

JIM: Well, mostly off-Broadway, but she was lucky enough to earn the role of Harper in Tony Kushner's *Angels in America*. So yeah, she's now an official Broadway actress.

DR. SOW: Well, that explains why everyone here constantly talks about her, regardless of the incident. I hope everything works out between you two.

JIM: Thanks.

(DAVID enters from stage left. He is a Caucasian man in his mid-30s. He swats a fly as he enters.)

DAVID: Damn bugs!

JIM: Uh, David, when does the tour begin?

DAVID: In a few minutes. How's Mrs. Powers? *(He quickly takes a glance at his watch.)*

JIM: She's feeling better, but still blind.

DAVID: I assume she's not coming, then.

JIM: Yeah, there's no way she's gonna be up for that.

DAVID: You know. This wouldn't have happened if she had followed the rules. I specifically told everyone not to wonder off the trail.

JIM: I know. I don't know what she was thinking.

DAVID: In any event this tour must go on. *(To DR. SOW.)* Does she need a doctor with her at all times?

DR. SOW: No, but I think it's best if —

DAVID: Good. Because after what happened yesterday, I need you on the tour.

DR. SOW: Fine, but I advice that someone stays with her.

JIM: Hey, if she stays, I stay.

DAVID: Good.

(LANA and FREDDY enter from stage left. They are a newly-wed couple in their mid-20s. They hold hands, while approaching the others.)

LANA: Hey, David?

DAVID: Yeah, what is it, Donna?

LANA: *(Politely correcting him.)* Lana.

DAVID: Oh, right. Sorry.

LANA: No problem, um…isn't this where the Tokoloshe supposedly lives?

DAVID: The what?

LANA: The Tokoloshe. *(DAVID shrugs to the others.)*

DR. SOW: *(To DAVID.)* It's a mythical creature, a common legend among these parts. It's like a…a Bigfoot, only smaller.

LANA: *(Excitedly.)* So, this is the location?

DR. SOW: Unfortunately, yes. Didn't think many Americans would have knowledge of it.

FREDDY: Yeah, you'll have to excuse my wife. She's a fanatic when it comes to folk-tales and magic.

DR. SOW: Well, if it does exist you wouldn't want to encounter it, but then again according to the legend, it can only be called upon by someone who's…who's wicked; traditionally, a witch. In other stories, however, it'll be someone who is…seeking vengeance. The creature can become invisible if it consumes a small pebble, and there are other stories in which the Tokoloshe can articulate all languages. They can even speak in several dialects and gain a personality of their own. That's one way how they lure their victims into…well…it's not very pleasant. *(He chuckles.)* Scientists who are intrigued by the legend have even made theories of why the creature behaves the way it does.

LANA: And what's the reason?

DR. SOW: It has no companion.

JIM: *(Sarcastically.).* Very interesting. And do you believe in it?

DR. SOW: I believe it as much as I believe hogs can grow wings, Mr. Powers. However, the tale has frightened many residents in Cape Town. Some parents don't even let their children out after eight because they believe the creature only comes out at night…and —

DAVID: And blah blah, yada yada yada. *(To Group.)* It's just a legend folks! No need for panic! *(To DR. SOW.)* Enough with the ghost stories, we have to get going. *(To Group.)* Alright everyone, get yourselves together! We're about to start the tour!

(DAVID exits stage right along with LANA and FREDDY.)

PAULA: *(Offstage.)* JIM?!

JIM: Yeah?!

PAULA: I would like some help here! I need some fresh air!

JIM: Be right there! Doc, can you give me a hand, please?

DR. SOW: It'll be my pleasure.

(They both walk upstage and into the tent.)

JIM: *(Offstage.)* Okay, we're right here, sweetie.

DR. SOW: *(Offstage.)* Grab her other arm.

PAULA: Ouch!

JIM: Sorry, babe.

(All three of them exit the tent. PAULA is a Caucasian woman in her late 20's. She wears a blindfold. JIM and DR. SOW guide her to the chairs and slowly sit her down.)

PAULA: Thank you, Dr. Sow.

DR. SOW: You're very welcome. Well, I must be going. Now, David forgot to mention this, but if the camping alarm goes off by any chance, the two of you must get into the nearest tent and remain silent. We'll hear the sound of the alarm and be back in minutes. No need to worry. Most likely nothing is going to happen, but just in case something does you know what to do.

JIM: Okay, thanks, doc.

(DR. SOW exits.)

JIM: Can I get you anything to drink?

PAULA: I don't know. <u>Can</u> you?

JIM: *(Sarcastically.)* Very funny. <u>May</u> I get you anything to drink?

PAULA: *(Rudely.)* No, I'm fine thanks.

JIM: Why are you acting like this?

PAULA: Why do you think I'm acting like this? I mean, it's pretty damn obvious.

JIM: It's not like you're permanently blind. You'll get your sight back.

PAULA: It's not only that, Jim. I never wanted to come here in the first place. The only reason why I'm here is because <u>you</u> wanted to be here. Even before I read the brochure, I had no interest in this place. Africa? Please! Who wants to roam around in the jungle in this heat? It must be over 100 degrees out here. *(She scratches herself.)* And let's not forget the insects.

JIM: I knew you were gonna bring this up. And you're acting as if it's my fault that you're blind. It's not. If you had listened to David earlier, none of this would have happened.

PAULA: Let's face it. We're not exactly the 'happy married couple' any more. Everyone else here seems to be. Look at Freddy and…Rhonda or whatever her name is.

JIM: Those two are a poor example, sweetie. They just got married for crying out loud. They're not gonna know what real marriage is until after the honeymoon. Watch, in a couple of years they'll be just like us. In fact, I think there's already some tension between them.

PAULA: Happy marriages have lasted a lot longer than ours, Jim.

(JIM walks behind her.)

PAULA: Where are you?

JIM: I'm right behind you. I found a pair of glasses on the ground. Probably belongs to one of the tourists.

PAULA: *(Sarcastically.)* Well, I don't think it belongs to any of the animals.

(JIM gives Paula a disgusted look.)

PAULA: And don't give me that look. I may be blind, but I can still read your mind.

JIM: Listen, I'm tired. I could definitely use a nap. Do you wanna go back inside?

PAULA: *(Disgustedly.)* No. I need some air. Enjoy your nap.

JIM: Are you sure you wanna be out here by yourself?

PAULA: It's better than being cooped up in there all day.

JIM: Alright. Well, if you need anything or if you're feeling uncomfortable, holler.

PAULA: Fine.

JIM: I love you, Paula. *(He waits for a response.)* Paula?

PAULA: I love you, too.

(JIM walks upstage and into the tent as the lights fade to black.)

SCENE 2

(Lights are up. The tour walks through the jungle. DAVID, without interest, is leading them.)

DAVID: And if you look to your right, you'll see some trees. And if you look to your left, more trees. And if you look down, no trees. And if you look up, you'll see my dreams floating away.

(LANA and FREDDY are the last two. THEY stop for a moment.)

LANA: Why are we stopping? David said not to stray from the group.

FREDDY: I just wanna have a little time alone with you.

118

(They kiss. She then pushes him away.)

LANA: We should really continue on.

FREDDY: C'mon, we're not that far behind.

LANA: Freddy, I don't wanna end up like Mrs. Powers.

FREDDY: *(Sarcastically.)* Yeah, I mean that makes sense. Who'd wanna be a Broadway actress?

LANA: You know what I mean.

FREDDY: C'mon, just one more kiss.

(She gives him a quick kiss.)

LANA: Let's get going.

FREDDY: I don't understand.

LANA: What?

FREDDY: Why did we pick this place?

LANA: Because I've always wanted to travel to another continent.

FREDDY: But why Africa? Why not someplace in Europe like…like Paris or Rome? A romantic spot.

LANA: You don't think this is a romantic spot?

FREDDY: Let's just say it's not really considered as a honeymoon spot. At least, not a famous one.

LANA: It's different. That's why I like it here. It's not the typical spot almost every other couple travels to.

FREDDY: Why must you always be so different? Why can't you just be…?

LANA: Normal? I tried that once, remember? At the wedding, when you gave me this ring.

FREDDY: Alright, let's just…catch up with the others.

(They exit.)

SCENE 3

(Lights are up. The VISITOR enters from stage right. He is a handsome looking man; an average representation of a girl's fantasy lover; roughly in his mid-20s. He steps on a branch as he walks towards PAULA. She reacts to the sound.)

PAULA: *(Gasps.)* Is someone there?

(The VISITOR only stares at her.)

PAULA: Hello?

VISITOR: Yes.

PAULA: *(Anxiously.)* Who are you?

VISITOR: I'm…one of the tourists.

PAULA: Shouldn't you be with the rest of them?

VISITOR: I decided not to go…haven't been feeling well. How are you doing? You must have been through hell.

PAULA: So everyone's been telling me. Yes, it was an experience I didn't need to go through and I still can't see a thing, but I'm no longer in pain. *(Beat.)* You're not expecting an autograph from me, are you?

VISITOR: I wasn't going to ask. But now that you brought it up, it would be nice. But like you said, you can't see a thing.

PAULA: Well, you seem very kind. Once I get my sight back, I'll give you one.

VISITOR: That would be great.

PAULA: I'm not the type that carries extra photos around, especially in a place like this. You wouldn't happen to have a playbill on you by any chance.

VISITOR: Nope…forgot it at home.

PAULA: *(Giggles.)* Didn't think so. That would be the perfect item for an autograph. But, considering we're in this kinda place, I guess a napkin or something will have to do.

VISITOR: No worries. It's not the item that makes it valuable. It's the signature itself.

PAULA: *(Smiles.)* You're very kind. *(Beat.)* Are you standing at the moment?

VISITOR: Yes.

PAULA: Have a seat.

(The VISITOR takes a seat beside her.)

PAULA: I didn't catch your name.

VISITOR: The name's…Travis.

PAULA: Paula. Oh, but then again you already know who I am. I keep forgetting how famous I am.

(They laugh.)

VISITOR: Well, it's a pleasure to meet a celebrity in person.

PAULA: You know. This would a perfect time to shake hands.

VISITOR: *(He takes a glance at his hands.)* Mine are pretty filthy.

PAULA: Oh…then perhaps some other time. Forgive me, but I do have a thing when it comes to dirt. It's amazing how I convinced myself to come here.

VISITOR: You don't like Africa?

PAULA: Quite frankly I despise it; regardless of my injury. I only came here because my husband wanted to. He's been dying to travel here.

VISITOR: Why do you think?

PAULA: Well, it's always been a childhood dream of his. As a child, he used to watch those National Geographic videos. And he loves animals. He practically knows every animal in the book. I don't understand why he decided to pursue a career in business. I mean he's good at what he does, but I don't think he enjoys it. He should have just stuck with science. Could've been someone like Dr. Sow. I think the chemistry classes got to him.

VISITOR: You must be a terrific wife.

PAULA: Not lately. I don't even think I love him anymore. *(She sighs.)* I shouldn't even be telling you this considering I just met you, but…I'm thinking of divorcing him…when we fly back to New York.

VISITOR: You sure you wanna do that?

PAULA: The romance is gone. There's nothing left in our relationship. He works days, I work nights…and days. He's off on Sundays, I'm off on Mondays…if lucky.

VISITOR: You guys are together, now. You might as well enjoy it.

PAULA: We've been fighting here as well. It's just not working out. *(Chuckles.)* Boy, I can just see the headlines now: 'Famous Broadway Actress Gets a Divorce,' 'Famous Broadway Actress Gone Blind' or even better 'Famous Broadway Actress Returns from Africa as a Total Mess.'

VISITOR: I'm sorry you're feeling this way.

PAULA: Don't be. I had it coming. I'm sorry, I don't mean to spill out my guts. Let's talk about something else.

VISITOR: Sounds great.

PAULA: So, where are you from? Judging by your accent, you're American.

VISITOR: Yes…I'm…also from New York.

PAULA: I picture you to be quite handsome.

VISITOR: I guess you can say I'm good looking.

PAULA: You single?

VISITOR: Yes.

PAULA: If I may, are you looking for anybody?

VISITOR: *(Chuckles.)* Why? Are you interested?

PAULA: Maybe.

VISITOR: *(Dumbfounded.)* Uhh…now…what would your husband think if he caught you saying that?

PAULA: To be truly honest, it'll be quite convenient.

VISITOR: What if I told you that he's standing right behind you as we speak?

PAULA: He isn't. I know for a fact that you're just teasing. I don't need eyes to sense where my husband is. But like I said, it would be convenient.

VISITOR: So, you <u>are</u> interested in…in…dating me?

PAULA: Sure. Why not?

VISITOR: Even though we just met?

PAULA: I'll get to know you as the days go by. I already admire your presence.

VISITOR: And you don't even know what I look like.

PAULA: I won't be blind forever. Besides, appearance doesn't matter to me.

VISITOR: I think you're bluffing when you say that. True, appearance isn't everything, but it's the first step towards attraction…in my opinion at least.

PAULA: I don't believe in 'Love at first sight.' Personally, I just think of that as a physical attraction. You don't have sexual relations with them because of their personality, but because of their looks. Just like a one-night-stand.

VISITOR: No offense, but I find your theory appalling.

PAULA: I'm not saying it's true. It's just the way I believe.

VISITOR: An actress, especially from the stage, should believe in 'Love at first sight.'

PAULA: Sorry, I don't do Shakespeare. I'm more on the contemporary side.

VISITOR: Yes, but when you look at it, 'Love at first sight' is quite self-explanatory; falling in love with someone you meet for the very first time. We only met a couple of minutes ago and already you want to date me.

PAULA: Very true, but there's just one little flaw in your theory: I'm blind. And besides, just because someone asks you out, doesn't necessarily mean they're in love with you.

VISITOR: But still, you should know what he's going to look like before you commit yourself to dating him. You weren't blind when you met your husband, correct?

PAULA: Of course. You're probably right. But let's say hypothetically that I don't get my sight back, that I remain blind for the rest of my life, what then? I would still wanna be with someone. And my urges wouldn't change. I would still have the desire to touch, and to kiss and of course…to fuck.

(The VISITOR stands up overwhelmed.)

VISITOR: You're going to fast with this. As much as I'm flattered that you have these feelings for me, I don't think they're pure. You're a married woman, Paula; a blind, married woman trying to seduce a complete stranger.

PAULA: You're not a stranger. I know your name.

VISITOR: *(Laughs.)* You know my name. That doesn't mean anything.

PAULA: I know we just met, but there's just something about you that I'm drawn to. Can't quite explain it. Could be your voice, your kindness, I don't know what it is. All I know is that I cannot wait to finally see you with my own eyes.

VISITOR: No…you don't.

PAULA: *(Confusedly.)* I'm sorry?

VISITOR: I'm not who you think I am.

PAULA: *(Not listening to him.)* Oh, my God. I think I can –

VISITOR: Everything I've been telling you about myself is a complete lie.

PAULA: Wow. Travis, I can –

VISITOR: That's not even my name.

PAULA: I can…I can see, Travis. Oh, finally, I can see again.

(As PAULA removes her blindfold, the lights fade to black while the VISITOR backs away.)

SCENE 4

(When the lights are up, PAULA no longer wears the blindfold and the VISITOR is offstage for the rest of the performance.)

PAULA: Wow. Oh, it's so great to see again. *(She looks around for him.)* Travis…Travis? Where are you? Travis?

VISITOR: I'm sorry, Paula. I cannot let you see me.

PAULA: Why ever not?

VISITOR: I'm nothing like you imagined.

PAULA: I already told you, I don't care about looks. I demand you come out here and show yourself! Don't you want my autograph?

VISITOR: You don't understand. You have no idea what you've been talking to.

PAULA: <u>What</u> I've been talking to? You're acting as if you're not human. Travis, I know this is gonna sound crazy, but I fell in love with a voice: your voice. A voice that has made me feel so comfortable inside. Something I haven't felt in the longest time with my own husband. All I wanna do now is finally see you with my own eyes. Please, Travis. Don't leave. Or at least don't disappear, yet. Not until I've seen you... Travis, please.

VISITOR: Fine. I'll reveal myself to you. You really want to see what I am?

PAULA: You know I do. Show yourself now!

(*Bushes rustle. The sound is possibly coming from the back of the audience. PAULA walks downstage facing the audience. Something catches her eye, creating her to express fear.*)

PAULA: Oh, my God. What are you?! Stay where you are! Don't come any closer!

(*She screams. The camping alarm goes off. JIM runs out of the tent. PAULA runs to JIM and embraces him.*)

JIM: What the hell is going on!

PAULA: I don't want to be here anymore!

(*DR. SOW, DAVID, LANA and FREDDY enter from stage right. DAVID exits stage right to kill the alarm. Once the alarm is off, he enters again.*)

DAVID: (*To JIM.*) What the hell happened?

JIM: (*As he sits PAULA down.*) I don't know. I was in the tent, I heard my wife screaming and then the alarm went off.

DR. SOW: Oh, Mrs. Powers, you can see again.

PAULA: After what I just saw, I wish I was still blind.

JIM: (*Kneels beside her.*) What happened, sweetie? What did you see?

PAULA: I can't even explain it...it looked so grotesque...so terrifying... it wasn't human. (*Beat.*) David...is there a Travis in our group?

DAVID: (*Checks the list.*) Nope. No Travis here.

PAULA: The whole time...the whole time, it was here...talking to me. Oh, Jim...I pictured him to be so handsome...so...so beautiful, so pure. His-its voice was so soothing. Oh, my God. I need to get out of here. Oh, Jim, I don't care if we have our differences. All I know is that

I want to go back to New York; to our own home. Please, Jim, I want to go home! *(She weeps into his arms.)*

JIM: It's alright, sweetie. We will…we will. *(To Group.)* Can someone please take her into the tent for me?

PAULA: No! Don't leave me.

JIM: I'm not leaving you. I need to talk to the doctor alone.

PAULA: I'm not crazy, Jim.

JIM: I know you're not. Please, can someone take her?

LANA: *(Holds PAULA's hand.)* Come on, Mrs. Powers, it'll be alright. We're here for you.

(LANA walks with PAULA to the upstage tent and they enter it.)

DAVID: That's it. No more celebrity tourists. *(As he exits.)* And with any luck, no more tours.

(JIM and DR. SOW remain onstage.)

JIM: Well, doc, what's causing this?

DR. SOW: I'm not a psychiatrist, Jim. It's definitely not one of the symptoms from the plant. I believe she did see something…maybe not a monster, but something.

JIM: You don't think it's the…?

DR. SOW: What, the Tokoloshe? *(JIM nods.)* No. Like what I said, it can only be called upon by someone who's vengeful. *(Beat.)* Oh, for heaven's sake, Jim. It's only a folk tale. Something like that just doesn't exist. Now, if you'll excuse me I'm gonna go check on her.

JIM: Okay. Thanks, doc.

(DR. SOW enters the tent. JIM remains onstage by himself.)

JIM: I guess there are just some things you don't know, Doc.

(He reaches for something out of his pocket: a handbook. HE glances at it and smiles.)

JIM: I think my revenge is complete. Paula won't be leaving me anytime soon. Hell, she may even have to spend some time in the clinic. That's what she gets for being unfaithful to me. But as much as she deserves this punishment, I will still be there for her, forever and ever.

(Bushes rustle. JIM faces the audience and smiles.)

JIM: You may go now…Travis. You've done your part. Better than what I expected. Who would've known you'd turn out to be a gentle giant, or should I say gentleman. I guess all legends have their quirks.

VISITOR: I hate being called upon.

JIM: Oh, I know you do and I apologize for that. It will never happen again. But I would still like to thank you for all your help.

VISITOR: What do I get in return?

JIM: What would you like? A companion, I know, but that I cannot give you.

VISITOR: I would just like to be invisible. The way I felt when I spoke to your wife. During that moment, I was not a fear. Only when I'm seen, am I a nightmare. I want to disappear. I want to not exist.

(JIM takes out a small bag of pebbles.)

JIM: I hear you eat pebbles.

VISITOR: They are hard to find in these parts.

JIM: Well then, take these. I've collected them throughout my time here; a lifetime supply.

VISITOR: Thank you.

JIM: No. Thank you. Here ya go. *(He tosses them offstage.)* Enjoy.

(JIM walks back upstage towards the tent. LANA comes out.)

JIM: How's she doing?

LANA: I think she's feeling a little better. What's going on with her?

JIM: You're asking the wrong person. Thank you for your help.

LANA: You're welcome.

(JIM enters the tent, leaving LANA by herself. She walks over to the pile of wood and is about to start a fire when something catches her eye. She faces the audience overwhelmed.)

LANA: Oh, my God. It's you.

VISITOR: You know who I am?

LANA: Of course I do. You're the Tokoloshe.

VISITOR: Why aren't you screaming?

LANA: Why should I scream?

VISITOR: Paula screamed.

LANA: So, it was <u>you</u> who frightened her.

VISITOR: I never meant to.

LANA: I knew there were some faults in the legend. You're not a monster at all.

VISITOR: You don't find me scary?

LANA: No. I don't. I'm intrigued by you, regardless of how you look.

VISITOR: You are?

LANA: Yes. You're the main reason why I came here on my honeymoon. So I could search for you, and I have. I've found you.

126

VISITOR: I'm glad I've made you happy. Perhaps I should –

LANA: No. Wait. Please don't go.

VISITOR: I cannot be here. The others I will frighten.

LANA: Then, take me with you.

VISITOR: What?

LANA: I know you need a companion, and I'm willing to be yours.

VISITOR: But you're married. I can see the wedding ring from here; sparkled by the sunlight.

(She removes the ring from her finger.)

LANA: I was forced to marry. Only because reality got the best of me, but when I'm here, I'm home. I love Africa…and I love the legend. I wanna learn more, more about you.

VISITOR: What's your name?

LANA: Lana.

VISITOR: You have a very pretty name, Lana; a name that I'll easily remember. Lana, would you like to explore the jungle with me?

LANA: Of course I would.

(She drops the ring on the ground and exits. FREDDY enters, looking for her.)

FREDDY: Lana! *(HE reaches center stage.)* Honey!

(He looks down and discovers the ring. He picks it up and looks out to the audience as the lights fade to black.)

THE END

ABRAMOVIĆ by Kory French.

ABRAMOVIĆ

By Kory French

Kory moved to New York in 2009 to earn a Master's of Arts degree from Columbia University where he studied the history of American Blues, Jazz and Rock n' Roll. Following a thesis called *The Subway Sessions* that examined the cause and effect of privately consumed music in public space, Kory went on to cofound two music-related companies: one in tech, and one in publishing. Kory has a Bachelor of Arts Degree from Acadia University ('00) and has done post-degree work at Queen's University ('07) and the University of Toronto ('08).

In the early 2000s, Kory engaged in a solo journey around the World that included at least 3-months traveling through every continent (save Antarctica). During that time, Kory wrote his first short novella (unpublished) as well as much other material that he has yet to develop into anything concrete. Upon returning to Canada, Kory completed his first full-length screenplay that has never been shopped.

Professionally, Kory works as a strategy and operations consultant in New York (4 years) for a company he began in 2011. He is also the host of a radio talk show that airs weekly on BreakThru Radio focused on rising authors and musicians.

Kory comes from Toronto, Canada, and this is his first play.

Abramović made its New York City debut on August 17, 2013 at the Hudson Guild Theatre. It was a semi-finalist in The Riant Theatre's Summer 2013 Strawberry One-Act Festival with the following cast, in order of appearance:

MARINA ABRAMOVIĆ	Ash Straw
SAM	Michael Hauschild
DEWEY	Adam Couperthwaite
PATRON #3	Steve Liskiewicz
PATRON #4	Meg Mark

PATRON #5   Alex Spieth
PATRON #6   James McCormick

The play was directed by Nicholas Hulstine.

CAST OF CHARACTERS

MARINA ABRAMOVIĆ, the Performance Artist. A Prima Donna, looking extravagant, yet mournful. She will sit silent and motionless for the duration of the performance.

SAM, a twenty-something male still unsure of himself. Somewhat fresh to New York, he is too cool for mainstream America, yet too naïve for New York's esoteric Art scene.

DEWEY, SAM's visiting best friend. MOMA's out-of-place harlequin.

Extra players. Three MOMA visitors who wait their turn to sit with ABRAMOVIĆ.

PATRON #3, a high-art male in this thirties.

PATRON #4, an Oprah-abiding young female in her twenties.

PATRON #5, an elderly man.

SCENE 1

(The towering Atrium located inside the MOMA (New York) in May 2010. Bright klieg lights accent the vacancy of a grand space in which two armless, oak chairs are set facing one-another, six feet apart, at Center Stage. The surrounding walls and floor are tall, bare and smoky white. Seated in the chair at Left Center is MARINA ABRAMOVIĆ. She appears like a timeless canvas in a large, over-flowing red concert gown with an extensive train. Her long, brown hair is in a braided plait and pulled forward over her left shoulder. Her skin is an odd, pasty white. She is slightly bent forward and stares intently straight ahead with her arms resting gently in her lap. She will remain in this position, motionless, for the entire performance, more as a part of the set than a player.

There is a line of waiting MOMA visitors horizontally upstage. MUSEUM PATRONS #3, #4 and #5 are the first three in line followed by MUSEUM SAM, holding a folded New Yorker, *and MUSEUM DEWEY. An airport security-line belt separates the PATRONS from the performance space with an opening at Upstage Left. The chair opposite ABRAMOVIĆ is empty. Lights.*

After a brief moment of silence and stillness, PATRON #3 approaches the vacant chair, sits, stares into the eyes of ABRAMOVIĆ and doesn't move.)

DEWEY: So that's it? She just sits there and doesn't move?

SAM: Pretty much.

DEWEY: How much is she getting paid for this?

SAM: Actually, I have no idea.

DEWEY: Well, I bet it's a lot. I mean, look at this place. Pretty damn nice looking. And a lot of people too. I can't imagine she would be sitting there for anything less than ten grand.

SAM: I doubt it has anything to do with money. It's a statement. In fact, I guess it's more of an invitation to be a part of something, isn't it.

DEWEY: Well, whatever it is, it just doesn't make that much sense. Some old lady all dressed up in red, sitting still while a bunch of randoms line up just to sit across from her? Half my town's been out of work for over two years and this broad makes a couple of G's to sit in a chair. This city-art shit annoys the fuck out of me.

SAM: You don't get it.

DEWEY: What's there to get? What are you gonna do up there?

(SAM shrugs, ignoring the question. There is an awkward silence. SAM turns to his New Yorker magazine.)

DEWEY: How does she go to the bathroom? Think she just pisses herself? What if you get up there and it reeks of piss? What if she actually shit herself? Man that sucks.

SAM: Even if she did, it could smell a lot worse. It has before.

DEWEY: What the hell does that mean?

SAM: *(genuinely edifying)* This one exhibition she did, she sat on a pile of rotting, bloodied cattle bones that were crawling with maggots and feces in some tiny, concrete dungeon like the ones you see used for solitary confinement. She just sat there for six hours a day, in the dead of the summer heat, scrubbing the bones clean with a brush while singing Montenegrin folk songs and telling stories of her childhood.

DEWEY: *(pensive)* Why the hell would you ever want to do that?

SAM: Trying to make a statement I guess. Some say she was performing an act of mourning for those who died in the Kosovo conflict.

DEWEY: That's a bit much, no? Whatever happened to laying a wreath on a grave or wearing a ribbon? Jesus fuck. This lady's nuttier than a squirrel in a shithouse.

SAM: Well that's exactly it. To her, traditions don't carry the same impact. Ya see with Abramović its all about limits—there is no faking it with her. If you want to capture the morbidity of war, you have to use real death things—its stench, what it looks like, the feel of it. Symbols and recreations won't cut it. On stage, a knife is a prop. To Abramović, a knife is real. And she'll cut herself just to prove it.

(PATRON #3, stands, leans in, and kisses ABROMOVIĆ on the forehead sincerely. He then turns and exits Stage Right. PATRON #4 approaches the empty chair and sits. The remaining 3 PATRONS in line shuffle forward.)

DEWEY: Well that guy gave up kinda quickly, didn't he?

SAM: Maybe it was just to say he did it.

DEWEY: Right? Maybe he's one of those artsy New Yorker fags who's can't wait to run home and blog while sipping on his ristretto venti nonfat organic chocolate brownie frappucino extra hot with foam and whipped cream upside down double blended.

(SAM stares at his friend blankly. Shocked, appalled, Impressed and amazed all in one.)

DEWEY: What?

SAM: We don't use that word here.

DEWEY: What word?

SAM: The "F" word.

DEWEY: What F word? Fag? You're telling me I can't call somebody a faggot now? Dude, did you see that guy? He had homo written all over him! He reminded me one of those German dudes we used to watch on SNL. Remember that skit? Starring, uh, Mike Myers and, uh, what the hell was that other guy's name?

SAM: *(Forgetting political correctness for a moment, he laughs at the innocence of his friend and fond childhood memories.)* Sprockets. Fuck, I forgot all about that. "Nowze de time on Shprockets ven ve dance."

DEWEY: Yeeess brother! Now that was some funny shit. That's what I call New York City performance. Not this "weird-ass-pretend I'm a mannequin" crap. Why couldn't you take me there? Why aren't we lining up for Saturday Night Live tickets instead of lining up to see some old lady shit herself?

SAM: Look man, you were the one who said you wanted to see something unique. Something you don't get at home. You watch SNL every week. This—this is something you're not gonna see anywhere. How are you not impressed? Imagine sitting in a wooden chair for seven hours a day, six days a week, over two and a half months. Think about it dude. Think about the discipline, the focus, determination. And the whole time you're inviting people to interfere with that space. She's seen people cry, she's stared at famous people, people from her past have come to surprise her, hell—even one guy came in, sat down, stuck his fingers down his throat and vomited all over himself! Imagine sitting there and witnessing all that, and not moving. It's extraordinary!

DEWEY: Mehn. I'm not that impressed.

SAM: You're not that impressed.

DEWEY: Nope. Not that impressed. *(Beat)* I could do it.

SAM: *(A short, disregarding laugh.)* You could do it.

DEWEY: I could do it.

SAM: Dude you couldn't sit st—

DEWEY: *(Interrupts.)* I'm telling you dude, I could do it.

SAM: *(Continues.)* You couldn't sit still for more than 1 hour. Guaranteed.

DEWEY: Oh yeah? Guaranteed?

SAM: Yes. Guaranteed. *(Beat)* In fact, I will bet you dinner tonight that you can't stand motionless for the rest of our waiting time. Until we get up to the front. Until it's my turn to go next.

DEWEY: I totally could. *(Beat)* But it's a stupid bet.

SAM: Why?

DEWEY: Because dummy—what happens when the line moves? Am I supposed to just stand here like an idiot while you move to the front?

SAM: You don't want to sit with her anyways. So head over there in the corner, and start standing still. Don't move a muscle. When my turn sitting with Abramović is over, I will come and get you. You do that; you win the bet.

DEWEY: Fine.

SAM: Fine.

DEWEY: Fine.

SAM: Fine.

(The two friends shake hands, laugh and playfully jeer one another. DEWEY removes his jacket and walks to a corner Downstage. He selects a goofy,

mocking pose, sets himself, takes a deep breath, and locks in. SAM observes him for the first few seconds, and then turns to his New Yorker magazine. DEWEY tries to watch SAM and ABRAMOVIC without moving. After about 30 – 40 seconds, he begins to falter. 15-20 seconds later, he concedes and returns to the line.)

SAM: *(Unsurprisingly laughs.)* Dude. You didn't even last a minute. I guess it's like sex for you, isn't it.

DEWEY: Yeah, well she gets to sit. Give me a chair and I'm golden. It's much harder to do standing up.

SAM: Right.

(PATRON #4 begins to softly shuffle in her chair. Eye-locked with ABRAMOVIĆ, she begins to wipe tears from her own cheeks. She is silently weeping. She breaks her stare, reaches down for her purse, and exits.)

DEWEY: What the fuck was that all about? She was crying? That lady just made her cry? But she hasn't even moved!

SAM: Transformation of emotions, I guess.

DEWEY: Dude if you cry when you're up there, I'm gonna smack the shit outta you.

SAM: I appreciate the warning.

(PATRON #5 approaches the empty chair. The remaining 2 PATRONS shuffle forward.)

DEWEY: Jesus, look at this fuckin' guy. He looks like he's fixin to die up there. *(Beat. Laughs to himself.)* I wonder if he died in the chair if she would snap out of her little trance?

SAM: Probably not.

DEWEY: Yeah right. *(Unexpected silence.)* Are you serious?! You really think if someone died up there she wouldn't move. Man, this is becoming borderline disturbing.

SAM: She herself almost died once and it didn't stop her.

DEWEY: For real?

SAM: Yeah man. *(Beat)* In this one performance she did, she lied down in a flaming star shaped out on the floor with sawdust and gasoline. After a while, the fire consumed all the oxygen and she passed out. Audience members had to jump in and drag her to safety. They saved her life. Her body was all torched, she burned all her hair off, fuckin' crazy dude.

DEWEY: *(Sincerely.)* Man—this woman is fucked up. I'm beginning to like her even more.

SAM: Another time, she placed something like seventy random objects on a table and invited the public to come and use any of the objects on her in any way they wanted. She just flopped around like a rag doll. People wrote on her, cut her, stripped her, penetrated her and one guy even took a loaded gun and held it to her temple while she just stood there not moving.

DEWEY: She put a fucking gun on the table! With bullets! And was like—"Have at it." And she never flinched!

SAM: Yep.

DEWEY: This woman's got some BALLS dude! Alright, you gotta explain this to me. I get that I'm just the out-of-town tourist here, but what is this lady looking for when she does all this whacked out shit? I mean, for real. And what are all these fucking people looking for? It's like watching a human train wreck.

SAM: Maybe you've hit something there. Why do we enjoy tabloids and self-destruction so much, like the demise of Lindsay Lohan? The downward spiral of Brittney Spears? The antics of Charlie Sheen? What is it about watching others fuck their lives up that intrigues us so much?

DEWEY: You think that's what she's on about?

SAM: I have no idea dude.

DEWEY: You should ask her.

SAM: Excuse me?

DEWEY: You should ask her. When you're up there. Just ask her.

SAM: You can't. Not allowed. You have to sit silent and motionless with her. It's part of the performance.

DEWEY: Ahhh, bullshit. What are they gonna do, kick us out? Who cares? Just ask her.

SAM: Yeah? And say what exactly? "Hi. What is the meaning behind your art?"

DEWEY: Just say, "What the fuck are you doing lady?"

SAM: Yeah, I think not.

DEWEY: Well, what are you going to do then?

SAM: I'm not sure.

DEWEY: Whaddya mean you're not sure. We've been standing in this line for almost three hours! You're like that guy at McDonald's everyone hates—stands in line forever and then doesn't know what the hell he wants when he's up at the counter. Fuck, I hate that guy.

SAM: Maybe I just want to look into her eyes.

DEWEY: For what Romeo? That lady's like, fucking, sixty. You better come up with something better than that. You're next! And Lord knows Andy Rooney up there's only got about four more minutes in him before he starts his afternoon nap.

SAM: Fine, maybe I do have something a little more exciting planned.

DEWEY: *(Giddy.)* Wait. Are you serious?

(SAM responds mimetically and mischievously.)

DEWEY: You sand-baggin' sonnuvabitch! What 'av you got planned?! HAHA! (howls disturbingly) I knew it! Come to show me some crazy lady sittin' still for hours fartin' and shitin' herself. Hells no! Whatcha you gonna do man?

(SAM smiles and continues to nod. He taps his breast pocket with a wink.)

DEWEY: What the fuck is that? What do you have in there? A water gun full of piss. No, no—a bunch of used condoms you're going to toss on her face. Forget all that, why don't you just whip it out man? Walk up there, unzip, and flop it out like a legend.

(PATRON #5 slides the chair back respectively and begins to get up.)

DEWEY: You're up dude. Make the boys back home proud.

(PATRON #5 exits. The intercom system at the MOMA begins playing "O Mio Bambino Caro" by Maria Callas. SAM waits until the singing starts before calmly and confidently approaching the vacant chair. DEWEY takes his cell phone out of his jean pocket and begins to record video of his friend, giggling excitedly in anticipation. SAM makes eye contact and his pretention turns to frustration. He remains standing behind the chair for a few seconds with both hands gripping the top of its backing. Then, with one sudden violent movement, he hurls the chair against the back wall with rage. ABRAMOVIĆ remains motionless. The lights go dark. Music continues with increasing volume.)

THE END

The Best Plays From The Strawberry One-Act Festival –
Volume Eight
Compiled by Van Dirk Fisher

SYNOPSIS OF PLAYS

FOOTHOLD by Patrick J. Lennon
A goofy Mary Poppins-ish nurse treats a shy man with an ingrown toenail and a broken heart.

WRITERS RETREAT by Samantha Ciavarella
Things get messy when you're the subject of your own story. Two friends/lovers/writers realize quickly that they cannot have their cake and eat it too.

A SONG A DAY KEEPS THE DOCTOR AWAY by Freddy Valle
A play about an ailment so embarrassing, you wouldn't tell your Mom about it. Say Aahhh.

WHERE'S THE REST OF ME? By David E. Tolchinsky
A screenwriter wrestles with his relationship to Spalding Gray, his psychiatrist father and the classic movie, King's Row. A dark and funny journey through movies, monologues and mental illness.

KIDS THESE DAYS by Rachel Robyn Wagner
Like the Brady Bunch . . . Only with drugs, alcohol, sex, and most of all honesty.

HOPELESS, IRRESISTIBLE by Keaton Weiss
Two strangers meet at a mysterious train station in an ambiguous afterlife, and force each other to confront their tragic pasts and shape their uncertain futures.

HOMECARE by Phoebe Farber
Homecare is a play that explores one woman's journey from anger and isolation to a deep desire to connect.

THE EXIT INTERVIEW by Betsy Kagen & MK Walsh
Before moving onto the afterlife, a young woman must participate in
an exit interview with an obnoxious celestial being.

PAULA'S VISITOR by Keith Miles Filangieri
What we see is beauty. What Paula sees is beast.

ABRAMOVIĆ by Kory French
As middle America continues with its economic struggles, a MOMA –
visiting Midwestern twenty-something tries to understand the monetary
value of high-art, grounding his friend in the process.

ABOUT THE AUTHOR

Van Dirk Fisher is the Artistic Director of the Riant Theatre and a graduate of the High School of Performing Arts in New York City and S.U.N.Y. at Purchase, where he received his B.F.A. in Acting. He has produced *The Strawberry One-Act Festival, My Soul Sings Too, Sister; A Play Festival Celebrating The Spirit of Women,* directed and written several musicals including: *Dream Babies, the musical about teenagers living in foster care and attending a charter high school, Somebody's Calling My Name, Sweet Blessings, Tracks, Loving That Man Of Mine, Rock-A My Soul In The Bosom Of Abraham* and *Revelations.* Plays include: *A Special Gift, Code of Silence, A Sin Between Friends, The Banjo Lesson, Mixed Blessings, Hotel Paradise* and *The Atlanta Affair.* Realty Show: *Who's Got Game?* An improvisational show in which 20 actors compete for the title of Best Playa Playa and a cash prize.
Mr. Fisher is the author of **LOVING YOU, *The Novel.***

Everyone wants a soul mate.
The hardest part is choosing between your heart and soul.

They said there would be no secrets between them. And there weren't. She just didn't tell Michael her lover's name. It wasn't important anyway, not now, because after today, she would never see Justin again.

Justin was preoccupied with Mariah as they stepped outside so he didn't notice the gray BMW parked across the street. He should have been paying attention, but he wasn't. All he could think about was Mariah. She loved him, and he knew it. She just didn't want to admit it, but he knew it. The CD by Darnerien was one clue. The fact that she didn't keep any photos of Michael on her desk was another. Oh yeah, Justin was full of himself. He thought he had Mariah pegged, but what he didn't know was that she kept Michael's picture closer than her desk. In fact, she wore his picture in a locket that she wore around her neck. Michael was the closest to her heart. Closest to the warmest part of her body that left her moist at night when she lay in bed alone thinking about him long after he had gone. Yes, Mariah was fortunate. She was loved by two men.

Available online at www.therianttheatre.com, www.barnesandnoble.com and www.amazon.com

To order the soundtrack to LOVING YOU go to www.therianttheatre.com. You can follow us on Facebook at www.facebook.com/loving.novel

You can follow us on Twitter at www.twitter.com/RiantTheatre. Like Us on Facebook at www.facebook.com/RiantTheatre, www.facebook.com/StrawberryOneActFestival and subscribe to us on YouTube at www.YouTube.com/Riant161

Printed in the United States
By Bookmasters